HOLIDAY TROUT FISHING

HOLIDAY TROUT FISHING

BY

H. S. JOYCE

Author of
"By Field and Stream," etc.

HERBERT JENKINS LIMITED
3 DUKE OF YORK STREET
ST. JAMES'S LONDON S.W.1

A
HERBERT
JENKINS'
BOOK

Second printing

THIS BOOK IS PRODUCED IN
COMPLETE CONFORMITY WITH THE
AUTHORISED ECONOMY STANDARDS

Printed in Great Britain by Wyman & Sons Ltd., London, Reading and Fakenham

FOREWORD

WHEN I started fishing for trout a great many years ago, I began to search for a cheap book that would give me the information I required without a mass of technicalities and that would be useful in any part of the British Isles. As time went on I continued to look for this book in order that I could present it to some of the young friends I have helped in the art. When I had passed my sixtieth birthday and was still without the book I wanted I decided to write it myself. Here it is. I hope it will be useful to you, and I also hope that it will help to increase the number of anglers who count their successes, not by the number of fish caught, but by the pleasure they have obtained.

H. S. JOYCE

TO PETER

CONTENTS

LIST OF ILLUSTRATIONS

HOLIDAY TROUT FISHING

CHAPTER I

THE PHILOSOPHY OF IT

I HAVE been fishing now for over fifty years and during that time I have caught nearly every species of fish in the British isles; those fish, that is, that inhabit or regularly visit fresh waters. I have not yet caught a sturgeon; I believe that only one specimen has ever been recorded as having been taken by fair angling in fresh water in this country. Nor have I ever caught a char; though it is really surprising how often I have noticed that my licence permits me to angle for this fish in districts in which it has never yet been seen nor is ever likely to be seen in the future. I can be quite as happy sitting in a punt in a lily-fringed mill pool waiting for a perch to bite as I can be walking beside a moorland stream, with the heather and bracken around my knees and the cry of the curlew in my ears, searching for trout. And with regard to the latter, most of the streams that I have fished have been of the half-a-crown-a-day variety; or, in other words, they have been streams open to the public on payment of a reasonable sum for the day, week, or month, as the case may be. I have therefore followed in the footsteps of the great majority of trout anglers in these islands and have rarely shared the companionship of the fortunate few who fish the more select and expensive streams of the southern counties.

In the course of my half-century of fishing I have gradually acquired a nice little collection of books on angling ; what angler hasn't ? Some of these books I have bought new, some I have picked up on second-hand bookstalls, and some (a great many I find) have been given me by kind friends. I value these books, not only for what they can teach me ; but also because in reading and re-reading them I am transported again in mind to the scenes and circumstances that have provided me with so much pleasure. But among all these books I can scarcely find one that deals adequately with the needs of the half-a-crown-a-day man. I have books on fly fishing in Scotland, in Ireland, in Wales, or in Devon ; I have some even that deal solely with that subject, ever so remote from the man of limited means and time, the chalk-stream trout. But I have none that could be rightly called a book on general trout fishing for the average man. It is because of this that I am now going to attempt to write a few chapters on what I consider to be the essentials for this class of angler. In the course of these chapters I hope to provide him with just enough information on equipment and method to make his short and necessarily cheap holiday a real pleasure and a successful venture, whether he should choose to spend it in Devon, Cornwall, Wales, Cumberland, Scotland, or Ireland ; or, for that matter, in any other part of these islands where cheap trout fishing is still available.

But, before I get down to materials and methods, I should first like to find out, and perhaps adjust, his attitude towards this delightful sport.

There was a time, and even I can remember it, when people counted the success of their trouting by the number of dozens of fish they could creel in a day. This can still be done in a few favoured and more or less remote localities ; but is it either essential or advisable ? I have never been keen on making heavy baskets. I don't know if I was influenced by early reading of *The Compleat Angler* ; old Izaak could catch two trout and then be quite content to sit beneath a hawthorn bush and chat with a friend, or watch the birds and admire the flowers. At any rate I soon discovered that the pleasures of a day's fishing was not measured by the number of fish slaughtered. Now I often limit myself to, say, half a dozen; and, when I have taken that number, I sit down and enjoy the scenery and wild life around me; or perhaps take out my pencil and book and make a sketch. Often when I set out to go fishing I say to myself, " I could do with three fish for ourselves for breakfast to-morrow." One can make a very good breakfast from a nine inch trout. I may get four; in which case I usually keep back one and have it cold next day with a bit of watercress—a very delightful breakfast; or so I think. I may have in mind a friend to whom I would like to make a present of a few trout; and so, should I succeed in catching six, I may give him three. I *never* give trout to those people who want a great heaped plateful. A trout is a delicacy, not only from the angler's point of view, but also (or so it should be) from the culinary angle as well. People who guzzle trout as they would a herring ought not to have the opportunity of eating them. If you want to know the value of a live trout, go to a Hatchery and ask their price for one hundred nine inch fish; you will then see that it is a creature that, apart from its own intrinsic merits, should be treated with the same respect we show to other highly priced articles. I hate to hear a fellow say, " I had a fortnight on the so-and-so. No Sunday fishing, unfortunately, and two days were too wet to go out. I fished ten days and took one hundred and fifty fish." To begin with, no one ought to want to fish for fourteen successive days; a break of at least one day in seven is good both for the fishing and the angler. And, anyhow, what on earth does anyone want with one hundred and fifty trout? The man who says that sort of thing has got an entirely wrong outlook on the subject. Besides, if you let loose half a dozen of these grab-alls on a river, what are the prospects for the half dozen reasonable anglers who take their rooms for the following fortnight. This kind of thing is an example of the competitive spirit, and the competitive spirit should never be encouraged in any form of field sport. It is perhaps an essential feature in athletics; but I discourage every symptom of it when it rears its ugly head in the most delightful of all pastimes. A wave of irritation passes over me when a fellow comes along and says, " Had any sport? I've had a dozen and a half." He doesn't want to know how many I have had; he is merely seeking an excuse to let me know how clever he is. I reply, probably untruthfully and, may be, a thought impolitely, " I've had a very good day. I've got two and that is all I require." I learnt that trick from a dear old angler; I have his copy of Stewart's *Practical Angler*. He still fished for trout when he was over eighty years of age and could catch them even then as well as anyone. He never took more than he required and to the usual inquisitive angler his bag was always the same, " Two," he would say and hold up two fingers. He would then stop fishing and enquire which way the other was travelling. Then he would direct him; " You go down and try that bit at the tail of the island. I'm going up to the top of the next pool. Good day ! " He said to me, " I go out for a bit of sport and a quiet smoke beside the river. I don't care if anyone else catches a cartload of fish, so long as he leaves one or two for me. And I don't see that it is any business of his how many fish I catch."

If you suffer from this competitive disease, get it out of your system as quickly as possible. Until you have learnt that the catching of fish is only a part of the joys of fishing, you will be robbing yourself of perhaps the greater part of the pleasure fishing is capable of giving to those who follow it in the right spirit.

Often when I have been spending a holiday at an angling centre the weather has been all against the the angler. Perhaps I have struck a really dry spell.

The other anglers moon about the place and grumble. I know that however low the water is there is always a fish somewhere that it is possible to catch ; and, if I fail, there is always something to be learnt by just sitting down in some sheltered spot and observing what is going on around. By this habit of sitting down and watching I have learnt much that I could not have learnt in any other way, both in connection with fish and also with the other creatures that live by the water.

A friend once said to me, " You always seem to see so many remarkable things when you go fishing." To which I replied, " And other people might do the same if they would only spend a little more time looking about them and not be for ever racing from pool to pool in an endeavour to beat the next man in the number of fish caught."

And now that I have shown you my philosophy ; or, as you may think, my foolishness ; you will know whether it will suit your taste to read on or to throw this book out of the window. If the latter, it matters not to me provided you have paid for it ; though I might hope that the window were closed so that you should have to pay for that also. But, if the former, then you and I will get down at once to the business of outfit ; for I see that we are well suited. I will not advise you on a great expenditure of money. I know that you are, as I am myself, but of limited means ; and, though a good article costs money and is always a good investment and usually cheaper in the end, there are ways in which a saving can be effected without loss in efficiency. I will even tell you how you may, on occasion, make satisfactory substitutes for some of the items of your equipment, and which will answer very well until such a time as your wife, pitying you, or perhaps herself, because your cigarette-tin fly-case compares unfavourable with those of your fellows, presents you at Christmas with a wonderful affair of aluminium and celluloid windows that will uphold your and her dignities when you sort out the contents in the hotel lounge next July or August.

So let us settle down now right away to the subject of rods, nets, reels, gut, and what-not. Then, when we have acquired all that is really essential, we will off to the river and see how we can best use our materials in the pursuit of our sport.

CHAPTER II

THE TOOLS OF OUR CRAFT

YOU will require a rod, reel, and line. You will require a good many other things ; but these three go together and really form one implement, and it is absolutely essential that they should balance. A line that is too heavy for the rod is a terrible infliction. It hinders the action, put too much strain on the rod in lifting, and its weight keeps the rod-top down so that good casting and quick striking are impossible. If its use is continued the rod will eventually develop a permanent downward curve. And a line too light is equally objectionable, though less likely to harm the rod.

I remember once meeting a fellow on sick leave from the Army during the 1914–1918 war. He had come down to Somerset for a quiet spell in the country and had decided to occupy himself in trying to catch a few trout. His doctor, himself a fisherman, had advised this, well knowing that there is nothing better to soothe the nerves and calm the mind than the concentration necessary in the occupation of trout fishing. The shell-shocked soldier had gone to a recognised sports outfitting establishment, told them were he was going, and asked them to fit him out with equipment suitable to the district. I was filled with indignation to think that a man in his condition should have been so shamefully misled. His rod was very short and rather stiff, and his line was of the finest silk; so fine in fact that it blew about all over the place. With that stiffish rod the only possible method of getting the line to take the fly out on to the water was to stand with one's back to the wind, hold the rod well up, and let the line float out on the breeze. He said that he had caught no fish and found it very difficult to cast. I told him that I could not possibly catch trout with the rod and tackle he was using. He refused to take my rod; but asked to be allowed to watch me for a little while in order to see how it was done. I caught several trout and then got him to promise to meet me next day at the local tackle shop, when I would select material suitable to the type of water he was fishing. I fitted him up and a day or two later met him again, when he told me that he was fully satisfied with his new purchase and had already taken several fish.

For the rod I recommend a built-cane of eight or nine feet. Many people will tell you that there is nothing so sweet to handle as a greenheart. This is quite true; but a greenheart is liable to dry off and will then snap. A broken rod-top is not a very serious affair when you have the river always at your door and almost certainly a spare top in your room; but a break during an all-too-short holiday is a much more distressing happening. I have used the same eight-foot built-cane trout rod for nearly thirty years and have met with only one accident, when I carelessly let a door slam on the top joint. This rod is very light and on the whippy side; but it has killed fish up to five pounds in weight—salmon, sea-trout, trout, and chub—and could probably tackle fish of double that weight. I gave six guineas for this rod; so that, including the cost of the new top, it has cost me less than five shillings a year. One cannot cast quite so far with a light, whippy rod as one can with a stiffer, heavier weapon; but I am sure the lighter article is much more generally useful and I consider it much more pleasant to handle. Though one may have to leave some fish that may be rising on the other side of a widish stretch which one could have covered with a stiffer weapon ; when one comes to the small waters, where a short line and neat cast is required, the little flippy rod scores every time. Besides, with my little rod, even a four-ounce fish gives me some very exciting moments.

The reel should nicely balance the rod. If it is too heavy, the weight will swing about under your arm as you cast ; and if it is too light, you will soon find that you need something to steady the rod. I prefer a fairly large reel, say of three inches in diameter, of light metal and with a big drum, to a smaller one of heavier metal and with a small drum.

The line should be of dressed silk and level. Don't be bothered with a tapered line ; you can get all the taper you require by a careful gradation of the thicknesses of gut lengths in your cast. And see that the line brings the rod-top nicely into action when there is eight feet of free line beyond the point.

The rod, reel, and line should all be bought at the same time ; or, if you already have the rod, take it with you to the shop and see that you get the other two articles to suit it exactly. Don't rely on the shop-keeper, or his assistant ; they may be only salesmen and have no practical knowledge of fishing. If you are not an expert yourself, take someone with you who does know something about it, and get him to try the outfit before you pay for it.

The next of your requirements is gut. I prefer to tie up my own casts, and for this purpose I get a supply of lengths in sizes 2X, 3X, and 4X. You can, of course, obtain the casts ready made up ; these are usually two and a half or three yards in length. I never make up a cast to be longer than six feet, and for small streams I use a cast of only four feet. Supposing I am using gut lengths of twelve inches, I make up my cast by using three lengths of 2X, two of 3X, and two of 4X. This allows for the loss of one foot in tying and gives me a nicely tapered cast which, when I get hung up in a bush, will usually obligingly break at the last two lengths; so that it will be necessary only for me to tie on one, or at most two, lengths of 4X, attach another fly, and carry on. A cast that is made up of gut lengths of the same thickness throughout may break anywhere; most often I find, within a few inches of the line. This means, the loss of a whole cast, instead of merely a point; and this is annoying, wasteful and extravagant.

Keep your lengths of gut in the dark. Don't ever carry a spare cast round your hat; although this may look sporty and may be a convenient place in which to keep it. Light seems to be gut's worst enemy. " Shammy " leather is about the best material in which to keep gut. I made myself a wallet with pockets for the different sizes of gut lengths. In this I keep all except the few lengths that are in my tackle book. Good gut lengths kept in this manner can be relied upon to last two years, which is twice as long as it can be *relied* upon to last under any other method of keeping that I have ever tried.

Gut substitute, though it is almost useless for fly-fishing for trout, comes in very handy for various purposes. I always use it for spinning traces, worm tackle, etc. It is cheap and, for a short time, very strong, but it requires to be watched carefully, as it is inclined to rot if it remains damp for too long. No gut should be used in a dry state. When dry it is brittle and snaps even when one attempts to tie it, so get a cast damper. This is a flat, round box containing one, or perhaps two, pieces of felt or flannel. Before setting out to fish, damp the flannel and place the cast you intend to use between it, under it, or even on it. I always prepare two casts; the favourite is placed on top of the flannel, and the spare beneath. I also put in two lengths of 4X gut, so that they will be damped ready for the time when the inevitable bush or tree claims its dues from my tackle.

Your first duty at the end of your day's fishing is to remove these casts and gut lengths (if there are any left) from the damper, so that they will not rot by having to remain there until the next time you go fishing.

You will require a landing net. My advice is that you never go out without a net. The fish may be small and a net may seem an unnecessary load, but in every stream there are a few out-sized fish, and one day you will get attached to one of these fellows. If you have left the net at home you will never cease to regret it, as it is unlikely that you will get a second chance for a considerable time.

There is no such thing as the perfect net for all occasions. You may have one that can be hung over a strap across your shoulders, so that it rests against your hip. The handle is about two feet long and this is a very useful net when one is wading, or when the banks are not steep. There is a long-handled net with an iron spike at the end of the handle, so that it can be used as a wading staff, very handy in a rocky stream, but the thing is cumbersome when travelling. My favourite is a telescopic net. It hangs through a metal ring in a strap across my shoulder and with it I can reach out to a distance over weeds or down from a steep bank. It has one disadvantage : one has to remember to extend it fully, otherwise the tapered shaft does not grip and the net itself is liable to turn round in swift water. It packs up into a small space for travelling.

See that the bag of the net is deep and the mouth wide. Better to have a net too large than too small. The net is to help in the capture of the larger fish, and there is no saying how large they will be. A shallow net also may let one down badly, for one cannot always be certain that the fish has given its last leap when it is in the net. I have seen more than one fish jump out of a net with a shallow bag, and on several occasions I have rendered assistance to someone whose own net was too small to deal with the monster he had hooked.

Some sort of a bag or basket is needed. The old-fashioned wicker creel has never been surpassed, but it is an awkward thing to pack. A waterproof bag with two compartments is the general favourite nowadays, but you cannot drop your fish into it with the same ease as you can drop them through the little hole in the lid of the wicker creel. I always have " hare " pockets in the tails of my fishing coats. Very often I do not bother to take a bag, but I carry a clean cloth with me, in which I wrap any fish I may catch and drop the parcel into one of my " hare " pockets.

You have now all the really essential articles with the exception of flies. I will deal with them in a separate chapter.

CHAPTER III

ATTEMPTING THE IMPOSSIBLE

I PROMISED I would leave the subject of flies to another chapter. This implied that the matter could be dealt with in a chapter. But to do so fully would require a volume, and a very much larger volume than the present. However, bearing in mind a story I once heard, I think it can be discussed with sufficient completeness in the space I have allowed myself. The story was told me by an old friend who gave me my first lessons in catching trout. His father had been a well-known North Devon angler and had kept a fishing-tackle shop in a part of the county very attractive to angling visitors. Many of these visitors came to his shop for their tackle. When he had put up his shutters at the end of the day, it was this old gentleman's invariable custom to take down his rod and go for a stroll beside the river. There he often met and conversed with those who had paid a visit to his shop earlier in the day. One such person had met him every evening for a week, and on each occasion he had inquired what flies the old man was using (in those days everyone used three flies on his cast). The reply was always the same. At last the visitor exclaimed : " I have now met you every evening for a week, and you have been using the same three flies on each occasion. Don't you ever use any others ? "

" Well, sometimes I do, but not very often. I put those three flies on at the beginning of the season, and I shall probably go on using them till I lose them in a bush."

" But when I came to your shop and asked for some good flies you showed me scores of varieties, and I bought several dozen of about ten different sorts, all of which you said were good."

" And so they are, perfectly good flies."

" Well, why don't you use some of them yourself ? "

" I do. I am sure I recommended these three to you. They are the three best flies I know, and if the fish don't like 'em, they don't know what's good for 'em."

The story was told me because I had expressed my doubts about ever being able to remember all the different varieties of flies required for the different times of the year and different types of water, and it was to show me that I could get along very comfortably with quite a small stock of flies and of very limited variety.

One can spend an enormous amount of time changing flies, and all this time has to be taken out of the day's fishing. I have always found it rather a troublesome business to change my fly. One has to break off the fly to be discarded, pick out the end of gut from the eye, put the fly back in its place in the box, select another, thread the new one on, tie the knot, and cut off the end. All this takes a great deal of time.

On reaching the station one evening after a day's fishing, I found there a man who had been fishing in front of me all day. On comparing results I discovered that I had a dozen good fish, whilst he had only one.

I had been using the same fly all day. The other asked me to show him this wonder-working fly. It was really nothing very original—merely an ordinary Blue Upright, with a turn or two of silver tinsel in the body. He begged me to give him one to copy and he told me that he had tried thirty-two varieties of flies during the day. Now, just calculate how long it takes to remove and tie on thirty-two flies. Though he started fishing an hour earlier than I did, I must have spent nearly twice as much time fishing ; whilst he was messing about changing flies, I was catching fish.

And this reminds me again of my old teacher. I asked him, " What fly do you consider catches most fish ? "

His reply was, " The fly that is oftenest on the water."

I once knew an old working man who was a very keen trout fisher. He never used more than one fly and that fly was always the same—a Blue Upright. He dressed these flies himself and always used a rusty-grey feather. This rusty-grey feather is not easy to get, but I was lucky to spot a fowl with this coloured hackle hanging up in a poulterer's shop. I bought the fowl and lay in a good store of feathers which enabled me to tie as many of this type of fly as I required.

If I were limited to the choice of six flies, I should select the following : Blue Upright, Greenwell's Glory, March Brown, Red Spinner, Black Gnat, Wickham. This selection provides something pretty nearly resembling any sort of fly one is likely to meet with anywhere ; and though the locals may tell you that it is quite useless trying with anything but the particular local fly, don't get depressed about that ; just put up the nearest you have to it, and I shall be surprised if you don't get fish.

If you have these six flies in two sizes, you really have twelve varieties, and it will be some time before you need bother yourself with others. Of course, I know quite well that you will purchase a few of the local favourites wherever you are ; everybody does that. But I want to make it quite clear that you needn't feel that you *must* have a more extensive collection before you can hope to catch anything but a very occasional fish. I rarely have more than six different sorts of flies with me when I go off on a fishing holiday, and I find that I generally manage to do quite as well as most others ; at any rate, I am sure I get quite as much pleasure.

If I were allowed to add three more flies to my selected list, I should choose Coch-y-Bondhu, Pheasant Tail and Alder. The Coch-y-Bondhu is a good illustration of what I may call a substitute fly. The creature is, I believe, supposed to represent the Bracken Clock, a beetle found only where bracken grows. Quite apart from the fact that I can't see any resemblance to a beetle in the Coch-y-Bondhu, it will kill fish in water where the beetle it is supposed to represent has rarely, if ever, been seen. I nearly always put it on when the river is fairly full and somewhat peat-stained.

It is rather more than likely that you will fall to the attractiveness of the winged fly as against the rather un-fly-like appearance of the simple hackle fly. But my advice is, don't. There is really nothing in it. The winged fly looks more like the natural insect to you ; but does it do so to the fish ? I very much doubt it. Nearly all flies have transparent wings, and it seems to me that the light coming through the separated strands of a hackle fly must make it look very much more like the natural insect than the winged fly with its opaque wings. Another point : as soon as you have caught a fish on your winged fly, or even after you have used it for an hour or so, it loses its trim appearance and becomes, in effect, a hackle fly. It now seems to have become really attractive to the fish. At any rate, I never use anything but hackle flies myself, and, if you should happen to see a winged fly in my box, you may be sure it is one somebody gave me years ago and which has probably remained there ever since.

When you are selecting flies, choose those on hooks with a wide gape. The wider the gape, relative to the size of the hook, the better chance you have of finding a hold that will stay put. I often make a fairly large hook carry a small fly by tying the fly almost in the middle of the hook shank. Although the finished article does not look particularly neat, I have a hooking power in it that I could never get with the usual 00 hook.

If you are likely to have any fishing after dark, one of the best all-round flies for the purpose is an Alder. Many people swear by the Coachman for night-work. It is an excellent fly for the purpose and, what is not so generally known, is a very good daylight fly when the river is rather full and the water somewhat peat-stained, particularly if there are any sea-trout about ; but I consider the Alder more generally useful, as it often does well by day even in quite low and clear water. Both are winged flies ; but whereas the Coachman has white wings, and so is supposed to be more visible to the fish by night, the Alder has dark wings, and, so many people think, is therefore not so visible. This is, I believe, a false argument. In both cases the wings are opaque and must therefore appear to the fish as dark objects against the light of the sky. I think that the " build " of the fly is of much greater importance in night fishing than the colour.

For further and more complete information on flies to use, consult the shelves of books and Tackle Makers' Catalogues that are almost without number.

CHAPTER IV

LET US DRESS THE PART

I AM not really fussy about my clothes; in fact, my family often complain that I go about in what they disparagingly refer to as "rags." My reason for this apparent neglect of appearance is that I cannot endure finding myself all dressed up just when a job comes along that may entail dirt, wet, and perhaps rather rough treatment of my garments. All these things may happen when one goes a'fishing; therefore see that your clothes are fitted to withstand any or all of these trials.

I once met a man trout fishing who was wearing a frock coat, a low-cut waistcoat with a starched "dickey," and a flat-brimmed bowler hat; the latter so aged that it was of a deep green tint. I think this was the most extraordinary outfit I have ever seen on the banks of a river. The reason may have been that the angler, being old and having perhaps passed the age when he might have required these garments for some state occasion, had decided to wear them out on the banks of his favourite stream. The bowler hat at any rate may have proved of more use than merely to protect his head from the heat of the sun—I have known one come in handy for use as a landing net when the proper article did not happen to be available. But I should not affect such a dress from choice. The chief points to remember with regard to clothing are that it should be inconspicuous, comfortable, and strong. If it is waterproof, that will be another point in its favour. It should also suit the temperature at the particular time of the year. There is little too choose between being boiled with heat or frozen with cold. Both are very unpleasant and both detract from the pleasures of angling.

My favourite outfit consists of stockings, Bedford-cord knee-breeches, a waterproof shooting coat, and a tweed hat with a fairly wide brim. The breeches are laced at the knee, so as to avoid the discomfort of pressing upon a button when crawling to a position ; a movement that is often necessary. The colour of the breeches is also a nondescript fawn, the coat being of much the same tint. The coat is furnished with plenty of capacious pockets. There are five pockets on the outside : one on either side of the skirt, one on either side of the breast, and a small ticket pocket on the right hand side just above the waist line. The skirt pockets have flaps ; but those in the breast have perpendicular openings and no flaps. Inside the garment there are four pockets : two very large " hare " pockets with washable waterproof linings, and two large pockets placed one on either side within the breast. With this liberal supply of pockets one can distribute one's tackle, lunch, etc., so as to avoid uncomfortable bulges and so that the weight is more evenly spaced. The coat is made very full ; so that, when thrown open during hot weather, plenty of air can circulate between it and the body and, by making use of its many pockets, there is no necessity to further burden oneself with a bag or basket, the strap of which will considerably increase one's heat and discomfort. The inside breast pockets are important ; they should be wide enough and deep enough to take your boxes of flies. It is most unwise to place such relatively frail things as fly-boxes in a skirt pocket where they are liable to be crushed when one reclines for a rest, or to take one's midday meal.

The tweed hat is by no means perfect ; but I like it because it is so comfortable. Its chief defect is that it is not waterproof. I have tried a proper waterproof hat but have found it so terribly hot that I prefer getting wet in my old tweed. I think that the most serviceable hat would be an old trilby with a few holes punched around the sides of the crown ; but my trilbies usually fall to bits before they reach a stage when they could thus be converted into fishing hats.

However hot the weather is, do not be tempted to fish in shorts. Nettles sting, and brambles and thistles scratch and prick. The comfort of freedom about the legs will not counterbalance the discomforts of stings and scratches. Stones, also, can be painful to crawl upon when there is nothing between your bare knees and their rough surface.

Avoid loosely-woven materials ; they look very nice and sportingly rugged when they are new, but soon look little better than old pieces of sacking when they have passed through a few bramble bushes and barbed wire fences. Plus-fours catch every burr and thorn they pass and, after a shower or a scramble through wet herbage, are such a sodden mass of misery that I for one should prefer to disrobe and continue in my pants.

Many people wear flannel " bags " or " slacks," and there is no particular objection to them if one is also wearing waders. But if one is bank fishing I consider them messy, uncomfortable things ; they draggle in the wet grass about one's ankles and show every mark when one kneels in a damp spot. There is a theory that the colour is just right : being that which that clever fish-catcher, the heron, has chosen for his coat. I have not tested the theory, so cannot express an opinion upon it.

You will agree that my fishing clothes are well suited to the job they have to perform ; which job is to protect me from the elements, hide me so far as possible from the keen eyes of my quarry, and provide me with a handy means of carrying the necessary equipment for my sport and comfort during the day. I have tried and discarded a good many different types of garments and I do not think I can very much improve upon my final choice.

CHAPTER V

WITH CAT-LIKE TREAD

FOR as long as I can remember I have read that fish can hear, and with equal frequency that they cannot. The former contention is usually supported by a story of some fish that lived in a pond and were called to feed by the ringing of a bell. It was therefore laid down that one should not talk whilst fishing. I was told this when as a very small boy I went out simply as an observer ; but since then I have observed other small boys, and I have noticed that they are not usually silent in their observations ; quite the contrary, most of them ask a great many questions. This desire for knowledge is very commendable ; but I now appreciate that it can be very disconcerting to a man who wishes to concentrate on his fishing and at the same time does not wish to appear unkind to a small child. I should like to be able to say that it has been definitely proved that fish can hear : it is so useful to be able to say this in order to discourage talkative onlookers. Unfortunately it seems now to have been proved fairly satisfactorily that fish cannot hear, and by this I mean that they cannot appreciate sounds in the same way as we can. They can, however, feel, and in this faculty they are very much in advance of human beings ; for their appreciation of vibrations is much more sensitive than ours. So it all boils down to this : it is inadvisable to talk, because too much chatter is a distraction and fishing requires the whole of one's attention ; and it is definitely disadvantageous to tramp about on the bank or to do anything that will send a vibration into the water, because fish are extraordinarily sensitive to this sort of thing. Therefore at all times when fishing, or even when only spying out the water with an intent to fish it later, one should walk with the greatest care.

Since fish nearly always lie with their heads pointing upstream, it follows that one stands a better chance of approaching them unobserved if one does so from downstream. A careful approach in this manner will often reveal the presence of a good fish close under the bank ; an approach from the upstream side would probably have revealed your presence to him before you could spot him. He would then have slid quietly beneath the bank and all you would have seen would have been a very inviting spot that was apparently waiting for a suitable tenant.

And it is not only yourself that you should remember to keep hidden, there is also your shadow. If possible it is always better to fish facing the sun. This may be awkward at times owing to the glare that may be reflected from the surface of the water ; but it is almost impossible to find perfect conditions for anything in this very imperfect world—imperfect, that is, according to human desires—and half the interest would be taken out of fishing if it were made too easy. The shadow both of yourself and your rod must always be kept off the water you wish to fish, and this you must remember may mean not only the few feet or yards that lie right before you, but also perhaps the whole of the pool or shallow above ; for a frightened fish will often spread alarm for a considerable distance as he dashes away at your approach.

One afternoon I was out trout fishing and sat down on the bank to rest for a few minutes. Before me was a rather long shallow and I began to examine the bed of this in the hopes of locating a fish or two. I had spotted two lying close to the stones on the bottom, when suddenly a fish darted past upstream. The two fish I had spotted immediately took fright and followed. Other frightened fish dashed by, nearly every one of which disturbed another that had been lying unobserved by me close to the bottom. I peeped round the stump of an ash tree that grew close by to see what had caused all this disturbance. A man was wading up the middle of the stream. His long shadow travelled before him warning everything of his approach, whilst his rod, waving and shining above him, flashed additional warning signals. He came ashore when he saw me and sat down to talk. He had caught nothing and scarcely seen a fish; he thought there could be very few in the river. I did not like to tell him that he could scarcely expect to catch fish if he continued to wade about in the bright sunlight in the way he had been doing; nor did I tell him that I had three nice fish in my bag and expected to get another couple before I need go home. He could see that I was not wading and he would naturally suppose that, if he could catch nothing with that advantage, it would be most unlikely that anyone would do better who had to stay on the bank. There are, of course, places where it is impossible to fish unless you wade; but on the other hand there are plenty of places which, by the use of a little care and ingenuity, one can fish without entering the water. I never wade unless I am obliged to and I think I generally have my full share of fish. On the bank I run far less risk of disturbing water in front of me, and I have not the discomfort of struggling along like a half-dressed deep-sea diver.

An eye for cover is a great advantage. The fellow who hurries along from pool to shallow, and from shallow to pool, may cover a great deal more water and cast his flies upon it a great many more times than the fellow who walks along quietly, casting carefully and observing his surroundings; but it is unlikely that he will do any better. Cover that lies behind one and is high enough to prevent a silhouette of one against the sky is often of more advantage than cover that actually lies between oneself and the fish. In such positions I have often stood openly on the bank and watched fish without them noticing me.

It is often astonishing how small a thing upon the river

bank can be used as an effective screen from the eyes of
the fish. Only about a week ago I caught a beautiful
trout from a small stream by using a few tall sedges as
cover. The sedges grew so thinly on the bank that I
could see clearly between their stems, and there I saw
this trout poised between two clumps of waving green
weed. The fish was so close that I could almost have
touched it with the rod-point. It was much too close
to cast at ; so I just lowered my fly carefully down in
front of its nose. It was really rather absurd to see the
fish taking my fly so close to me ; but it was all very
exciting and interesting.

Where low bushes grow along the bank, one should
not stand over them in order to reach the water. The
further back one can stand (or kneel) the more chance
one has of getting one of the fish that almost certainly
lie just off this sort of cover. There is, of course, always
the risk of catching one's fly in the bushes or herbage as
one recovers it. This is annoying and may mean the loss
of a fly ; but it can often be avoided by lifting the fly by
a sort of outward movement of the rod, so that it rises
from the water almost straight upwards instead of at
an angle that cuts into the top of the bushes. I have
seen whole stretches of excellent water completely
ruined for several seasons by the removal of all the bank
cover. Fish like shade and never like being overlooked.
Also, insects like to rest in bushes and frequently miss
their footing when clambering about amongst the
branches ; the trout very soon get to know this and
haunt these places.

You will probably very soon meet with some learned
fellow who will tell you all about angles of refraction.
It is quite likely that he will suggest that it is absolutely
essential that you should know all about this ; in fact he
may hint that you cannot expect to catch fish unless you
do. Some people are like that ; you must do the thing
their way, or not at all. Actually it all amounts to this :
because of this remarkable angle a fish can see you before

you can see him. Not always, of course ; you have got
to get within his " circle of vision " before he can see you
and that gives you plenty of chances of spotting him
first in spite of this extraordinary angle. But at any
rate you ought to know that there is such a thing, and,
knowing it, all you have to do is just to avoid poking
your head over the bank just anywhere ; you may be
in a spot where the angle law works and that would be
just too bad.

Trees overhanging the river often afford wonderful
look-out places for fish observations. It is not usually
very much good trying to fish from them. Sometimes
one can dap successfully (of which more anon) ; but
one can nearly always learn a good deal about fish from
such a situation. I have spent many a profitable and
amusing hour stretched out on an overhanging bough,
or leaning against a projecting trunk. In such a position
one is usually quite protected by the leaves and branches
overhead, and one can watch the fish beneath without
any fear of detection, provided one makes no sudden
movement. The powers that fish have to appreciate
vibrations is readily seen should one's foot happen to
slip on the rough, curving trunk. The quiver that is
set up in the water may be quite invisible to the human
eye ; but the sudden departure of the fish is a sure
indication that it has not escaped their attention.

Sometimes, when the water is very low and clear, one
can crawl to a fish over an open gravel stretch. I have
frequently done this ; but I do not think that in every
case in which I have been successful it has been because
my approach has been unobserved. I think the fish
have seen me but have mistaken me for one of the cows
or sheep that come there to drink. I believe that trout
are often attracted to cattle by reason of the flies that
surround them ; at any rate I once circumvented some
particularly wily trout by taking my stand amongst
some cows that were in the river and casting my fly from
there. Unfortunately the cows took alarm when I

hooked a particularly lively trout, and they departed to their pastures leaving me without my cover.

Many of the best trout fishermen I have known have been small men. I think it was their lack of height that contributed considerably towards their success. A small man is less likely to show above the sky-line, and to adopt a crouching position for any length of time is very trying for a tall man. Fine and far off is an excellent piece of advice in trout fishing ; but low down and close to is equally good. I knew one man who always wore a leather knee-cap when fishing. I have done so myself at times. Rabbiting knee-caps suit this purpose admirably ; they can be obtained through almost any ironmonger or gunsmith. With one of these knee-caps on can crouch on one knee without fear of getting wet.

Wind can also be a very useful cover. When a sharp breeze is blowing I usually make my way at once to some open stretch of still water. Such a place can only be fished when the surface is ruffled by a breeze, or when the water is rather heavily coloured. Under either of these conditions it is often surprising how readily the fish take the fly. The explanation is, I think, that these fish are rarely fished for because they dwell in such an apparently impossible situation ; people look at them on a bright sunny day, sigh because they know it is useless to cast a fly over them, and pass on. But with plenty of ripples breaking up the surface of the water it is not at all difficult to approach and cast over them without being seen.

Where the bushes on the bank are thin enough to see through fairly clearly, it is a good plan to cast over them without allowing the head to appear above them. By peeping between the branches one can see what is happening to one's fly. A very much surer result can be obtained by first examining the place carefully from between the branches, locating a trout, and then fishing for that particular fish in the manner described ; this is a most fascinating way of taking a fish.

CHAPTER VI

IT LOOKS SO EASY

I THINK we shall have to hark back a little. I have sent you off to catch a trout and maybe you have found that this casting business is not half so easy as it looks. When you have managed to get your fly on to the water it is probable that the fly, the cast, and a great heap of line all landed together in a lump. You snapped off flies in the bushes behind you, you caught them in the trees overhead, and you even snapped them off in the air. Well, you mustn't expect to learn it all in five minutes ; but we will get out into the middle of the field, where there are no trees or bushes to get in the way, and we will try to get over the difficulty and at any rate learn to make a straight overhead cast.

To begin with, you must realize that your fly has to travel through the air as far behind you as you intend to cast it in front, and it must travel this course in a line without sharp angles. It was a sharp angle that snapped off your fly in the air. You heard a crack like the sound of a whip, thought something had gone wrong, and on examining your cast found that the fly had disappeared. You made the return cast too quickly, and that was the cause of your misfortune. But, you may say, when you linger over the back cast and give the line plenty of time to straighten out, you find that the fly falls to the ground and is caught on the tops of grasses. It is just the happy medium between the too-quick recovery that snaps off the fly in the air, and the too-slow return cast that allows the fly to fall amongst the grasses that you have to manage. The secret of attaining perfection in this is to rely on your sense of feeling. If you wave the rod about in the air, so that

B

the cast travels backwards and forwards above your head, you will feel a distinct pull on the rod-top when the cast reaches its extreme limit either way.

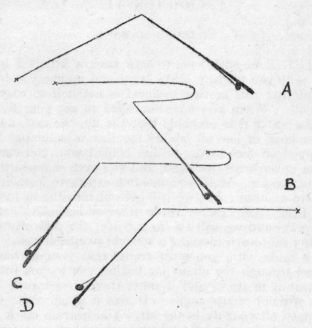

THE OVERHEAD CAST

Having practiced this backwards and forwards, waving of the rod until you can keep the fly travelling behind you and in front of you evenly and without dropping, the next step is to send the fly out so that it falls lightly upon the water with the cast and line in a straight line behind it. To get a perfectly straight line is not at all easy and only comes after considerable practice, but a reasonable degree of straightness is not difficult to manage, and fortunately you will begin by fishing in fairly swift water which will straighten out any twists or bends. To get the cast to fly out straight one has to "shoot the line." This is done by having a length of loose line, about two feet, between the left hand and the reel; then, just as the forward pull begins to be felt, this bit of loose line is released and the pull carries it out and allows the fly to alight in a natural manner on the water. It is best to practice this first out in the field, spreading a sheet of newspaper on the ground as a mark at which to cast. This is really all there is in the ordinary straight overhead cast, and this cast will enable you to cover any water in front of you provided there is nothing to hinder the flight of the line behind. But when you are fishing with trees and bushes behind you or on either side, it may be necessary to alter the direction of the backward flight of the line so as to avoid these obstacles. The oval track of the fly will now have to be bent upwards or sideways, as the case may be. In order to do this it is necessary to raise the point of the rod in an outward and upward direction instead of in an upward and backward direction, as is the case with the simple overhead cast. This outward and upward raising of the rod-point sends the fly and cast up in a perpendicular flight instead of in the more or less horizontal flight of the overhead cast; but it can be varied from the perpendicular through any angle till it reaches the horizontal in a sideways direction, according to the circumstances; it may be necessary, as when fishing under trees, not only to avoid obstructions behind, but also to avoid those at the sides. I think the diagram will make this fairly clear. These casts are much more difficult to make than the simple overhead casts.

One must be prepared to vary one's casts considerably when fishing thickly-wooded streams. I have seen some of the old Dartmoor anglers flip their fly in under bushes very cleverly. Taking the fly between the finger and thumb, they pulled the rod into the shape of a bow and then released the fly. I have never succeeded in becoming anything like expert with this cast. Sometimes the fly goes where I want it to go and as I want it to go; but more frequently the line and the fly land in a heap several feet short of the spot aimed at. But it is a pretty sight to see an expert do this trick.

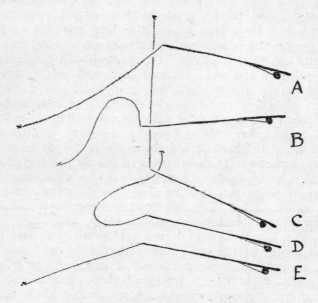

CASTING TO AVOID OBSTRUCTION BEHIND

I have met many anglers who have found it fairly easy to make a good cast when they have plenty of line out, but who cannot manage a neat short cast. The trouble here is nearly always in the make-up of the tackle. To bring a rod into action a certain amount of weight is required, and this weight is supplied by the line. If one is using a long gut cast when fishing a small stream, it follows that there can be very little line between the rod-top and the gut; consequently there is very little weight to help the rod do its work. I usually keep several gut casts ready in my book, ranging in length between four and six feet. A four-foot gut cast is quite long enough to fish with in a small stream ; and if on some very rare occasion I think an eight or nine-foot cast would be an advantage, I link on two or three feet of stouter gut to one of my six-foot casts. As a sort of rough guide I think one can say that there should be as much line between the rod-top and the gut as will equal the length of the rod. I know a very expert angler who does a great deal of night fishing for sea-trout and brown trout. He always pulls off exactly as much line as will bring the end of it to the bottom of his rod. He never varies this, and he is extraordinarily successful. When he wishes to reach a fish that is rising beyond his fly, he moves up until he can cast over it with his regulation allowance of line. I am not going to recommend this system because I get such a tremendous kick out of hooking a fish that has required all the line my rod can throw that I would not deprive you of the same pleasure. I merely record it because I think one can get any number of almost perfect casts by this method.

And this reminds me that I must warn you not to expect the impossible from your rod. A pliant rod cannot usually throw such a long line as one that is comparatively stiff. The very pliant rod reaches more quickly a stage when it can no longer easily lift and return the weight of extended line.

I was once told that I could not consider myself an expert trout angler because I admitted that I could only fish right-handed. The very superior person who said this probably considered that he was an expert and that there was nothing anyone could teach him about the game. Though, as already mentioned, I have been fishing for over fifty years, I am not a bit ashamed that there is still a great deal for me to learn ; in fact I think that is one of the joys of it. Some fresh problem crops up nearly every time I go out, so that there is never a chance of being bored. I admit that there have been many occasions when an ability to cast with the

left hand would have been an advantage. I can sometimes get the fly out fairly successfully with a left-
handed cast, but I find it difficult to hook the fish and
still more difficult to play it. I prefer to cast with
the right hand, but with the rod across the body and
over the left shoulder. It is, however, useful to be
ambidextrous in this as in many other things, and I
certainly recommend that you practice casting with
either hand.

It is, of course, an advantage to have the wind behind
one when fly fishing ; but in a very strong wind I prefer
to fish so that it comes across diagonally from the right,
and in this case I usually strike towards the left. This
may be only a personal peculiarity, but I mention it in
case you should find that a strong wind directly behind
makes it difficult for you to hook your fish. You are
almost certain to find that you have personal peculiarities that prevent you adhering strictly to what many
people consider the correct methods. Should the wind
be blowing directly in your face, it is usually an advantage
to keep the line low and to try and cast under it. The
ideal is a light breeze that ruffles the surface of the still
water and assists the angler in his casting. The other
extreme is a wind so strong that the fly refuses to
remain on the water. There is nothing that makes one
feel so futile as to see one's fly dancing about in the air
above the river and to be powerless to make it alight.
I know of no cure for this state of affairs. Rocks and
stone walls behind one are the most treacherous of all
obstructions. They seem so harmless, for there is
nothing on which a fly can catch. But when one has
missed three or four fish in succession, one begins to
suspect that something is wrong. A glance at the fly
reveals the distressing fact that the hook is like a poor
joke—it has no point. Without the angler being aware
of it, the fly has struck the wall behind and the hook
has snapped off at the bend. The golden rule, which
in the excitement of the moment I still so frequently

forget, is always to look well around you before attempting to fish in an unaccustomed spot. We learn by experience, and after repeating the same misfortune several times in a particular situation, we at length remember what we must do and what we must not do when we reach that spot. My first few days on a new stretch of water are generally much to the advantage of tackle-makers and the evidences of my misfortunes are visible on the tops of many bushes and trees.

CHAPTER VII

THERE ARE MORE WAYS THAN ONE OF KILLING A CAT

YOU have a fortnight's holiday and you intend to spend it in trout fishing. You had to fix on the date in January and there is little chance of getting it altered to suit the weather, because that would upset the holidays of the rest of the staff. You have arrived by the river and they tell you that they haven't had a drop of rain for a month and it looks as if there will be another month passed before any falls. The river is as low as it can be and gin-clear. Everyone says it is a waste of time trying to catch fish. What are you going to do about it ?

Well, it certainly won't be of much use trying to catch trout by the ordinary method of casting an artificial fly, except perhaps at dusk, or in the small trickles of broken water at the heads of the pools. But there is another method that is essentially a low-water, hot-weather method, and often a very successful one, and this method is by dapping.

If there are no restrictions in the Rules of the water in which you happen to be fishing against the use of natural insects, they are certainly better than the artificial.

It is not necessary that they should be alive ; nor does it seem to make much difference what insect is used, except in a few particular periods such as the grasshopper season, or the green caterpillar season. I have caught trout by dapping with bluebottles, or greenbottles, earwigs, woodlice, dung bobs, green caterpillars, wasps and moths. No doubt spiders would be excellent, but I am afraid of them.

If the artificial fly only is permitted, I consider the Coch-y-bondhu quite the best for this purpose. I think it is mistaken for a spider, and to me the creature looks far more like a spider than the beetle it is supposed to represent.

Dapping appears to be a lazy way of fishing, or at any rate a restful way. Actually I find it far more fatiguing than casting a fly. I spent about four hours at it one afternoon this summer and was completely finished by the time I packed up. My son considers it a great strain on the heart. One certainly lays oneself open to a good many shocks. There is a nice trout lying poised about mid-water under the bushes. The rod-top is carefully insinuated through an opening and the fly lowered towards the fish. The distance from the bank is a little too great to enable one to place the fly exactly in front of the trout, and it touches the water a foot nearer in. One's eyes were fixed upon the intended victim and the fly. Without any warning a monster of at least a pound dashes out from under the bank and grabs the fly. I defy anyone not to strike too soon, and of course that means a missed fish. It is absolutely necessary at this game to give the trout time to turn again towards the bottom ; otherwise one merely snicks the hook against the teeth in the top jaw. It is, of course, obvious that the strike in this method of fishing pulls the fly upwards and so directly away from the trout. In striking with a cast fly, the fly is pulled more or less parallel to the surface of the water, with the result that the trout is usually hooked in the side of the jaw. But unless the trout has got its head well down, this cannot happen in dapping, and the only part of the trout's mouth the hook is likely to come into contact with is the front part of the roof, which is quite the most impenetrable area.

It is advisable to use a hook with a good wide bend when dapping. A yard length of gut is sufficient, and a shot pinched on the gut a foot or so above the fly or bait helps considerably in keeping it steady, and makes it much easier to lower it through the bushes.

The most suitable place in which to dap successfully is where fairly deep water flows beneath well-bushed banks ; in fact the very places where it is usually almost impossible to catch a trout by casting the fly. Bush-fringed weir pools are often excellent spots and generally hold plenty of heavy trout. A stretch of a couple of hundred yards can provide one with several hours' fishing. With the sun in one's face, one can see the fish clearly and often select the best on which to try one's skill.

It is a slow process ; but the time passes with re-markable swiftness. Hasty movements and incautious approaches only alarm the fish and send them out into the pool or down under the banks. One creeps and peers between the leaves until one finds the sort of trout one wants ; then, very slowly, the rod is got into position and the fly lowered. Hitherto unnoticed twigs get in the way and adjustments have to be made in the amount of rod extended. Perhaps the fly gets caught up. Very careful shaking and lifting is required in order to free it without alarming the fish or getting into a worse mess. Often the trout misses the fly and the strike may send it up amongst the branches. It may take you nearly ten minutes to free your tackle. If the trout looks suspicious, leave it for twenty minutes and try elsewhere in the meantime.

Very often trout will rove along the sides of a pool and half a dozen well-placed openings will provide one with a full morning's fishing. When the trout are doing this, it is much better to limit the range of one's activities and get to know the peculiarities of each of a few openings. There are fresh difficulties to be overcome in every fresh place and one may save time, energy, and perhaps temper, by learning a few places thoroughly.

Some people may despise dapping and perhaps assert that little or no skill is required. " Just a poacher's trick " was how I once heard it described. I consider it very much more difficult to catch trout by dapping the fly than by casting. I miss quite three times as many fish when I am dapping. But I admit I shall never be really good at the game : I am too excitable.

I think it is advisable to use thicker gut when dapping ; 2X is not too stout. Often one hooks a heavy trout under circumstances where it is impossible to let it run and the fish has to be played on a tight line. Also it often happens that one cannot get a net to the fish because of intervening bushes. The creature has to be completely subdued and then lifted out. This cannot be done with safety on 4X gut. Since the gut does not touch the water and, even if visible to the trout, is mixed up with overhead silhouettes of twigs and branches, its thickness is not likely to scare them.

It is sometimes a good plan to vary one's methods when dapping. Sometimes it is only necessary to lower the fly till it touches the water, when it is at once seized by a fish ; but more frequently one has to suggest that the lure is alive by moving it gently. Dipping it repeatedly on to the surface of the water, in the same manner as the natural fly dips its tail repeatedly when laying its eggs, is perhaps the best method.

If a spider seems to be the desired bait, lower the artificial in a series of short jerks and raise it again when the trout approaches. By tantalizing the fish two or three times in this manner, as if the spider had recovered some of its thread, when the bait does at last come within reach, the trout will probably take it with a bang without first examining it and perhaps detecting the fraud.

If there happens to be another trout close by and the one you are after is inclined to hesitate, move the bait towards the second fish and one or the other is pretty sure to let jealousy or greed overcome caution.

A shy trout can often be induced to take a dapped fly by making the fly touch the water to one side and rather behind the fish. This is quite the surest way of catching a chub, " a very fearful fish," as Walton describes it. Let the fly hit the water with a pretty good smack a few inches to one side of Chevin's tail and he rounds upon it in a flash; drop it carefully in front of his nose and he will come to it carefully, inspect it, decide it looks a bit fishy, and sink out of sight. The same often applies to a trout.

So, on a hot day, when all the other anglers are moaning because they think fishing is useless, go quietly to some secluded, shady spot and dap carefully through the openings. You are sure to see one or two marvellous great trout and to have several moments of palpitating excitement. Also, you will probably catch one or two nice fish.

CHAPTER VIII

ONE MAN'S MEAT IS ANOTHER'S POISON

SINCE I have perhaps risked any reputation I may have had in the minds of some people by suggesting that you might like to try dapping as a means of catching trout on occasions when ordinary fishing seems hopeless, I may as well descend a few more rungs of the ladder of respectability and suggest that the worm can be a very killing bait.

I am not particularly concerned with worm fishing during a flood. Under such conditions very little skill is required. One has merely to drop the worm into an eddy, let it swing round with the current, and in all probability there will be felt at once the double " knock " of a trout taking hold. I consider it quite a legitimate way of taking trout, where the rules of the water permit it, and think that by its means a good many habitual bottom feeders are taken out of the water, which is quite a good thing, since such fish are unlikely to be taken on a fly. When fish are particularly needed and the river remains too high for a fly (though actually this is very rarely the case) a worm in an eddy will generally do the trick.

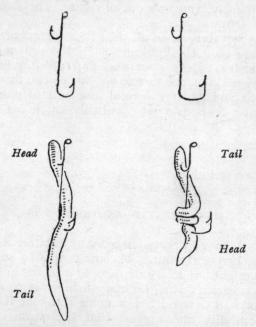

Head

Tail

Tail

Head

ALTERNATIVE METHODS OF ATTACHING WORM TO DOUBLE HOOKS.

But worm fishing when the river is at its absolute lowest is a very highly skilled art, and I can count on the fingers of one hand the number of real experts I have met. To become such an expert one must have perfect eyesight, a perfect sense of touch, and complete control of one's rod.

The method is to fish upstream, casting into the slightly broken water between rocks and where the stream runs into a pool, allowing the worm to come drifting down with the current. The angler must remain quite unseen by the trout, the worm must fall almost as lightly as a fly upon the water, it must travel at exactly the same rate as the stream without check or drag, and the angler must keep in constant touch with it. It is obvious that a great deal of practise is required to attain this degree of skill ; but once such skill is reached the results may be extremely good and a method of fishing is opened up for times when a fly would be of very little use.

Though three-hooked " Stewart " tackle is generally used and recommended, I have met clever worm fishers who used single hooks, and others who used " Pennell," or two-hooked tackle. One of the advantages of the three-hooked, or two-hooked tackle is that the worm is kept more or less straight and so has a more natural appearance. If a single hook is used, it is an advantage to have one with a barbed shank. In this case the head of the worm is pushed well up the hook and held in place by the barb on the shank, so that it hangs fairly straight. If a single hook without a barb is used, the worm is liable to slip down and form itself into an unnatural bunch at the bend of the hook. In all cases when fishing with a worm the point of the hook should be exposed.

I prefer to use a smallish, tough, pink-coloured worm, one about three inches long is perhaps the best size. I have often heard the dunghill worm recommended, but I cannot say that I have ever found it very successful. The suggestion that its scent is more highly attractive has been somewhat discounted by experimental evidence which suggests that trout have a very poor sense of smell. The late Garrow Green used to say that trout preferred worms taken from the soil around their own stream. This again seems to have been rather knocked on the head by the above-mentioned experimental evidence. All I can say with certainty is that worms, whether obtained from the banks of the stream or elsewhere, are all the better for being kept in damp moss for a few days before use, so as to make them tougher.

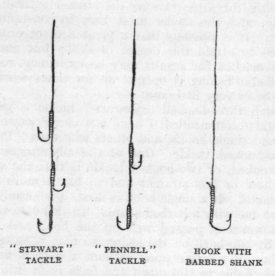

"STEWART"   "PENNELL"   HOOK WITH
TACKLE   TACKLE   BARBED SHANK

The addition of a single shot pinched on about six inches above the bait is another much-debated point. Some experts won't have it at any price ; they say that it checks the speed at which the bait travels and so renders its presentation unnatural. Others say that it sinks the bait down to the trout. It certainly makes casting easier.

The method of casting is by a sort of round-arm swing. If you cast the worm like a fly, it arrives in the water with rather a splash. If you cast it underhand it again is liable to come down with rather a splash and the gut will be, almost certainly, in a loose, wavy line. But with a well-timed round-arm swing the worm can be slung out so that it almost slides into the water, and the gut, line and rod will be as nearly as possible in a straight line between the bait and your hand. This is the perfect cast. The worm is now allowed to travel with the current and, so that one may keep in touch with it throughout its course, the rod point is raised, or, better still, brought round level with the surface of the water, at the same speed as that of the stream. This may sound rather difficult, but in actual practise it soon becomes comparatively easy. One gets into the habit of letting one's eyes travel down the stream at the same pace as the water is flowing, and one's hand keeps pace with one's eye. The difficult part is to hook the fish when it has bitten ; often the most difficult thing is to *know* when it has bitten.

A bite may be a " knock," a violent tug, or merely a checking of the bait. Since one cannot see what the trout is doing, it is difficult to give an explanation of these different types of bites ; and there is still so much to be learnt about fish and their ways that I prefer not to jump to a conclusion and find later on perhaps that it is incorrect.

Another difficulty is to know when to strike. Some tell you to wait a couple of seconds ; others advise striking at once. Not being an expert, I usually decide the point by trial and error. If I find that I miss fish by striking too soon, I give them a little more time. If I miss them by waiting, or they drop the bait after the first nibble, I strike at once. Sometimes the fish seem to be merely playing. They grab the bait and let go at once. No matter how quickly one strikes, or how long one waits, the result is the same. Any fish that is felt is merely "snicked" under such conditions. I believe that when this happens the trout are already fully fed and that they take hold of the bait just from force of habit, dropping it again when they find that they have no appetite to urge them to swallow it. The last word on a good many of these questions has not yet been written, and I don't think it ever will be, because I believe that the habits of fish are constantly changing.

There is sometimes an advantage in adopting the following procedure in clear-water worming for trout. Two styles of hook-flights are required, one with a small hook at the top and a medium hook below (say Nos. 2 and 4, new numbering), the other with a small hook at the top and one considerably larger at the bottom (say Nos. 2 and 7 or 8). In baiting the first, the head of the worm is fixed to the top hook, the bottom hook holds it about the middle, and the tail hangs free. If the trout are found to be removing the tail of the worm without being hooked, take one of the flights with the large hook at the bottom and reverse the worm by fixing the tail end to the top hook, passing the larger bottom hook through it midway towards the head, giving it two or three turns round the shank of the hook, and then passing the hook again through the worm nearly up to the head.

A roving trout can often be taken by a worm suspended just beneath the surface of the water. The movements of the trout should be studied and the worm introduced *after* it has passed upstream on its beat. The fish will probably pass the floating worm several times without taking any notice, but keep still and hidden. The temptation will eventually overcome its caution. When it seizes the bait, strike at once. It requires patience and skill to capture a trout by this means, and it is a very different thing from dropping a worm into an eddy during a flood.

CHAPTER IX

NIL DESPERANDUM

IN the last chapter I suggested that the water is rarely so high as to make it useless to try with the fly.

At one time I lived some miles from the river I fished and it was often quite impossible to find out the conditions before I reached the water. This river rose a good distance away upon the high moors, and though it might be brilliantly sunny in the meadows where I fished, it was quite likely that a terrific downpour was taking place up amongst the granite boulders at its source. These were the conditions when I reached the river one bright summer afternoon. The weather seemed so settled that I had prepared only to fish with fly; so I was definitely depressed when I found the water bank-high and the colour of strong coffee. There seemed to be nothing to do but to sit down and smoke a pipe. I went to a favourite pool and sat down under a tree. I was watching a large lump of white foam that was circling round and round in an eddy and thinking how closely it resembled a lump of rich cream upon a cup of coffee. Presently I saw a fine trout rise close to the circling lump of foam. A few moments later it rose again. I put up my rod, selected a fairly large fly, and cast to the fish. It rose immediately and I soon had it on the bank. I stayed by that pool the whole afternoon and took seven beautiful trout from around that lump of suds.

On another occasion on another river I arrived at the water unprepared for anything but fly fishing and found it in flood. Whilst watching the water I noticed a trout rising steadily close to the bank in an area of rather shallow water towards the tail of a pool. I caught that trout and, fishing similar spots along the river, caught several more. These experiences taught me not to despair when things seemed hopeless, and I have many times since had very satisfactory afternoons under similar conditions.

In the case of the lump of suds, I think that the trout find a number of drowning insects around such an eddy and cruise about in the neighbourhood, picking up what they can find.

In the other case I expect the trout are feeding on insects dislodged from the banks by the rising water. It would be difficult, if not impossible, for them to rise to these in the stream itself, as they would be swept away by the force of the current ; so they keep to the quiet water near the banks and search for such insects as may drift into such places.

A rather larger type of fly than that normally used is best for this kind of fishing, and my favourite is a medium-sized Coch-y-bondhu. Next to this I prefer a Coachman, which, after all, is only a Coch-y-bondhu with white wings. The Coachman is always looked upon as a night fly, and you are pretty certain to be scoffed at for using it by day. Don't worry about that ; use it and have the last and longest laugh, as you most certainly will if there are any fish about with an inclination to feed.

I have often taken sea trout when fishing with a fly during high and coloured water, and on several occasions I have risen and hooked salmon, though the latter have always managed to free themselves after a short attachment. A trout fly rarely gets a deep enough hold to enable one to land a salmon. The flesh tears with the weight of the fish and the hook drops out directly there is the slightest slackening of the line. But one day your luck may be really in. You hook a salmon on a trout fly, the fish stays in the same pool and doesn't indulge in too many fancy tricks. After half an hour of terrible suspense it turns on its side and allows you to draw it into the slack water near the bank. Perhaps your net isn't big enough to hold it. It may pay you to step into the water behind it, put your foot or your hand under it, and kick or throw it right out of the river. You may be able to " tail " it with your hand : a tricky business, in which you must remember to have your thumb towards the tail of the fish, not towards the head. You may also hook a finger into its gills. But, one way or another, you get the fish out. What does it matter if you are wet through to the knees ? You will be dry again in half an hour if you keep moving. What does matter is that you have killed a salmon on trout tackle, and that is an event of very real importance in an angler's life. The main thing to remember when you do so happen to hook a salmon is to keep cool. Don't put on too much strain and don't attempt to stop the fish if it decides to run. You will be surprised how much strain even a light trout cast will stand, provided the strain is steady. It is the sudden jerk that does the damage. Though I have yet to land a salmon on trout tackle, not one of the many I have hooked under these conditions have broken me : they have all come unstuck. But I have caught several when fishing for sea trout.

In almost every river there are long stretches of almost still water that are very difficult to fish under ordinary circumstances. When the water is clear the fish dart away in all directions as soon as you cast a fly over them. But go there when the water is full and coloured and fish in those parts that are only two or three feet deep. You will now find that there is just a nice current running. This will straighten out any curves in the cast and help to hide the gut. I always mark down such spots and go at once to them when the river rises. Many of the fish to be found in such places are above the average in size for that part of the river. Here, again, it is not necessary to roam far. It you have a suitable stretch before you, fish it up, then go to the bottom and fish it up again. You will perhaps discover in doing this that the fish have certain favourite spots. Each time you come opposite a certain bush you get a trout. You get only one at each visit and it seems useless to stay there and continue casting ; but when you reach it again in about an hour's time, there is another fish waiting for you. There are a good many things in the habits of trout still awaiting explanation.

CHAPTER X

ALL TROUT ARE CANNIBALS

ASSUMING that you followed my suggestions in the last chapter, I think I am fairly safe in assuming also that you met someone fishing with a minnow and that he looked rather scornfully at your fly and said, " You want a minnow when the water is high and coloured." You watched him throwing out his minnow and bringing it back towards him twirling through the peaty water, and you thought you would like to do that.

Fishing with a minnow is a very interesting method of taking trout ; but, unless you use only very light minnows not more than about an inch in length, you will find it difficult to hook trout on your rather light trout rod. You may get over the difficulty by having a stiffer and shorter top made for your rod ; or, if you have had the misfortune to break the top joint, you may discard the broken tip, whip the top ring on to the top of the remainder of the joint, and you will then have a very serviceable minnow rod. Of course you can buy another stiffer rod specially for minnow fishing ; but I have found a broken top joint perfectly satisfactory and do not feel the need to add to my already alarming collection of rods for almost every conceivable type of fishing.

Though your fly fishing line will answer well enough if you have no other, pulling it backwards and forwards through the rings all day will not do it any good, and it is really far better to provide yourself with another and a finer line. This line should be of undressed silk or cotton, and plaited—not twisted. The finer the line, the easier it is to cast a minnow ; but one must always remember that a very fine line is difficult to recover by hand. It certainly should not be finer than ordinary carpet thread.

Many shop minnows are, in my opinion, much too heavy. I have two favourites. One a little silvery fellow made of very light metal, and the other an invention of my own. The latter is my favourite. It is made from light copper tubing cut into lengths of an inch to an inch and a half. It has fins made of thin pieces of metal soldered on and bent in opposite directions so as to make it spin. It is neither coloured nor polished ; but it kills trout in spite of its rather dull appearance.

All my minnows are mounted on a flight consisting of a swivel, a short length of gut, a bead as a stop, and a single triangle at the end. Many shop minnows have no less than four triangles ; two at the tail and one at either side. These may catch fish that come at the bait side-ways ; but I think that this collection of ironmongery knocks off quite as many more and it certainly catches anywhere it touches.

Without including thread-line fishing, which really demands a complete equipment to itself, there are three methods of minnow fishing that can be followed using the ordinary trout rod and line. One is the " sink and draw " method, in which a weighted natural bait is used. It is possible to follow this method under almost any conditions of the river ; but it is most successful when the water is fairly clear and at normal height. Deep water should be selected and the minnow thrown out and allowed to sink. It is then raised a few inches drawn about a foot nearer in, and allowed to sink again Snap tackle is generally used, so as to enable one to strike directly a pull is felt. Many large bottom-feeding trout are taken by this means. The chief difficulty often is to obtain fresh minnows for bait.

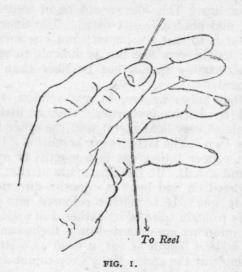

To Reel

FIG. 1.

1, 2 AND 3 ILLUSTRATING THE THREE STAGES OF SPINNING BY HAND

The second method is by spinning, and in this you have the choice of using either a natural or an artificial bait. The natural bait may be either fresh, salted, or pickled. (Salted or pickled baits may also be used in the "sink and draw" method ; though I have never found them anything like so good as the fresh bait.) Some people claim that the natural bait is much more killing than the artificial. This may be so ; but I find the artificial so much easier to carry and attach to the line that for a good many years I have used nothing else for spinning.

In spinning, the bait is cast out and its recovery effected by coiling the line into the palm of the hand. This looks very difficult ; but can be learnt in half an hour with a piece of string. Here is the idea : take the line between the first finger and thumb (Fig 1.) Turn the hand so that the little finger rests on the line two or three inches above where it is held by the finger and thumb ; (Fig 2), still pressing the line with the little finger, turn the hand down so that the little finger is now below the first finger and thumb, and grasp the line again by the finger and thumb at that part of it which is now brought level with them. (Fig. 3.) By repeating this movement over and over again, a series of loops is formed, and, as the later loops pack up between the finger and thumb,

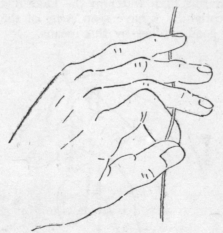

SPINNING BY HAND.   FIG. 2.

those made first fall into the palm of the hand, where they lie in neat order ready for the next cast. In casting, the loops are retained in the palm of the hand and a grip kept on the line by the finger and thumb until the minnow has swung forward. The grip being released at the correct moment, the minnow flies out and the line follows it neatly and without kinks from the coils in the hand. The fingers get tired at first; but in a surprisingly short time the action becomes quite automatic.

The third method really requires a specially long rod to be really effective. Its practice is chiefly confined to people who have always used the old-fashioned twelve and fifteen-feet rods. The bait is usually a natural dead minnow and the method of its manipulating differs from the others in that the amount of line in use during the progress of the bait through the water remains the same. A length of line about equal to the length of the rod is drawn off; the bait is swung out to its furthest extent and drawn through the water in a half circle simply by moving the rod round from the right or the left as the case may be. This is a very popular method of fishing during high water in the Lake district and in parts of Scotland. I have seen some of the old hands make very good catches by this means.

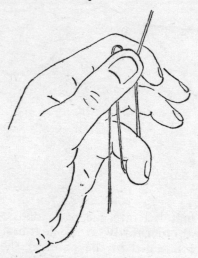

SPINNING BY HAND. FIG. 3.

All spinning minnows should be attached to the line by means of a gut trace containing at least two swivels

in its make-up. The gut need not be particularly stout ; though I prefer not to use anything thinner than IX. One usually has to strike harder to get a hold with a triangle than with a single small hook, and the trout itself often takes the bait with a considerable bang that puts a good deal of strain on the trace.

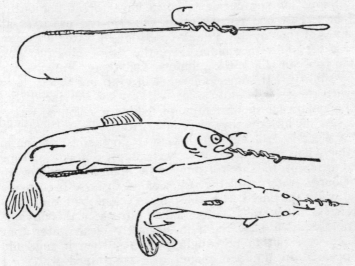

A SIMPLE TACKLE FOR SPINNING WITH A NATURAL BAIT ;
THE LIP HOOK CAN BE MOVED TO SUIT THE SIZE OF BAIT

It is quite a mistake to think that the spinning minnow can be used only in coloured water. A small minnow can be a very killing bait in low water ; but the water must be really low. I have often had good results when using it soon after daybreak when the river has been at its lowest summer level. Close to where I lived at one time there was a stretch of water which in periods of drought changed from a wide open stickle to a number of narrow channels between numerous rock ledges. Sometimes early on a summer's morning I would go to this stretch and, stepping from rock to rock, cast my smallest Devon minnow upstream and bring it down twirling through the narrow channels. It was " Town " water ; that is to say, all the inhabitants of the town had the right to fish there. Consequently it was very heavily fished ; but I have often taken half a dozen good trout from it in about an hour and a half before breakfast.

Supposing you decide to go in for a thread-line outfit, I have only one remark to make : Do not use it at all times of the day and in any condition of water. I know it is very jolly to wander along the river seeing just how far you can chuck the minnow, and there is always the possibility that some fool fish will grab hold of it, even when the river is quite clear. But I am convinced that this practice is spoiling minnow fishing in coloured water. I saw its introduction to a favourite river and watched its effects over a number of years. In the last season in which I fished that river it was almost a waste of time to attempt to catch trout on a spinning minnow in coloured water. All the fish seemed to have been made so well acquainted with the nature of the bait that they refused to lay hold. They had so often seen this obvious fraud twirled past them in perfectly clear water that they were not to be caught napping when it suddenly appeared in the semi-gloom of peat-stained water. I consider it an excellent method to use in tidal waters, and in such places I have taken by this means brown trout, sea trout, bass, plaice, and flounders. It is also very useful to use it to fish wide steady flats when the water is coloured. But I think it is definitely harmful to the fishing to go chucking a minnow about all over the river in perfectly clear water.

Perhaps you may have wondered why a " minnow " is used, though you know that in many of the rivers there are no natural minnows. The " minnow " may mean any small fish to the trout and in most cases is probably mistaken for a very small trout. All trout are by nature cannibals and eagerly devour any of their relatives who have the misfortune to be small enough to be swallowed.

Other methods of spinning the minnow are by the use of a " thread-line " reel, of which there are a great many varieties. By " thread-line " is meant a relatively thin line, usually either of silk or gut substitute, by means of

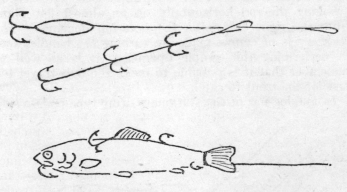

SNAP TACKLE FOR FISHING A MINNOW SINK-AND-DRAW

which and one of these special reels a very light minnow, or a plug bait, may be cast a considerable distance. In America the favourite seems to be one of the multiplying variety ; but in this country the stationary drum reel, in one of its many forms, is more generally used. In the multiplying and " Silex " type of reel the drum revolves parallel with the rod as in the case of the ordinary reel. In the stationary type the drum stands at right angles to the rod, so that the line leaves it without having to overcome the drag required to make the drum revolve. Some of these reels are fitted with ball bearings, some with adjustable or automatic brakes, some with a slipping clutch (by means of which one can so regulate the tension that it is impossible for a fish to break the tackle) and some with an automatic line distributor. They are rather expensive articles, costing anything up to five pounds or more. To describe all the varieties obtainable and explain how they should be manipulated would require a great many pages and is scarcely necessary, as most makers' catalogues give very full particulars.

When using a reel of the multiplying type, the cast is made direct from the reel itself, impetus being given by swinging the rod horizontally on an almost flat plane from the right or left as the occasion demands. The recovery is of course made by turning the handle, and, in performing this simple operation, it is as well to remember that it is possible to make the bait travel too fast for the trout to catch it.

In making use of the stationary drum type reels, a side

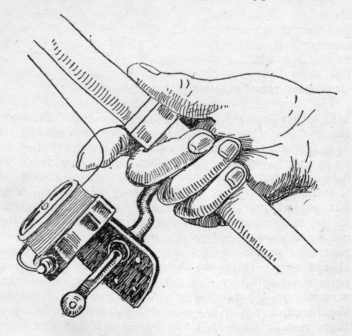

METHOD OF HOLDING STATIONARY DRUM REEL
BEFORE CASTING

flick is the usual method of making the cast, either from right or left ; but, when fishing between bushes, an overhead flick can be used. The action is somewhat different from that used with the revolving drum reel, where the swing is smooth and with a good follow-through. With the stationary drum reel the delivery is a rather quick flick.

It is usually better to fish upstream, or up and across ; and of course, when this is the method employed, it is very necessary to recover the bait sufficiently fast to keep it spinning. The edges of pools, the tails, the run-ins at the heads and under banks are the most likely places in which to find fish ; only occasionally will a fish take in the middle of a pool when the water is clear.

The chief thing to observe when using a reel with a stationary drum is to have the spool well filled ; the line then slips easily over the rim of the drum when the cast is made. Directly the bait ceases to exercise a pull on the line, which it does when it reaches the water, the line ceases to leave the reel ; and, since the drum is stationary, there is no over-run.

The diagram shows how my own thread-line reel is held at the beginning of the swing to make the cast ; the first finger is removed from the line immediately the flick is made. I use this reel only when fishing tidal water and have had some excellent sport with it. When fishing in rivers I much prefer the, perhaps, antiquated (I learnt it forty years ago from an old Dartmoor angler) but certainly very satisfactory method I have described in the earlier part of this chapter. Simplification does not by any means necessarily imply an increase in one's pleasure ; whereas overcoming difficulties most certainly always does. The more the results depend on my own personal efforts, the more pleasure I get out of any occupation. Though I don't play the fiddle, I fancy I should enjoy doing so, even if only moderately, more than manipulating the wireless to hear someone else playing even perhaps exquisitely.

CHAPTER XI

WHEN OTHERS SLEEP

MOST of my holidays have been taken in August. Before I took upon myself the responsibilities of a family I sometimes took my holidays in April or May, when I could enjoy some early trout fishing ; or I took them in October, when I could combine coarse fishing (I dislike that term ; often the fishing is as fine, or finer than trout fishing) with shooting. But August is the holiday time of the schools and I had to consider others as well as myself. August is not a good month for trout fishing ; but sea trout often give excellent sport at night and I am very fond of night fishing. It frequently happens that the rivers remain low for most of the month of August and daytime fishing is of very little use. It is, I think, the worst of the summer months for dapping and, though there still remains the clear-water worm and the minnow to try, I usually spend most of the day sketching and so am quite ready to change my brush for a rod when dusk begins to fall. Then, free from any worries and not having to trouble if I should feel sleepy next day, I can go to some quiet pool and thoroughly enjoy myself for an hour of two.

I have met quite a number of anglers who say that they have no use for night fishing. They say that they don't like blundering about in the darkness and that they find their line gets so terribly tangled. Most of these people have plenty of opportunities for daylight fishing. They can fish throughout the season at almost any time they wish. Consequently they regard night fishing as a disturbance to their rest and an inconvenient intrusion on their evening game of Bridge. But when most of one's season's fishing has to be confined to a fortnight of the year, with perhaps only an occasional afternoon or evening during the rest of the time, it seems foolish not to take advantage of any chances, even if they do involve cutting out an hour or two of sleep ; after all, one can make it up beneath the shade of a tree during the heat of the day, and what sleep is more refreshing than that ? As for the darkness ; it is rarely really dark in August, unless the sky is cloudy and there is no moon. And even then one soon gets accustomed to moving about in the dim light without difficulty or danger.

There is, I admit, a difficulty with regard to casting. One has to attain such a degree of proficiency as enables one to feel what the cast is doing. It is really a matter of paying close attention to what one is doing. Here, again, one's troubles are soon surmounted if one takes a little care in the initial stages to consciously feel the pull of the cast as it extends itself behind the rod. It is failure to do this that results in a " bird's nest." Provided one does not hurry the forward movement, giving time for the cast to straighten out behind, one should rarely get into any trouble. As a precaution, I always carry at least one spare cast ready made up. If I am wearing a trilby hat, I carry it wound round the band— the only occasion on which I carry a cast in my hat ; to do so during the day is to shorten the life of the cast considerably ; at night the gut suffers no injury. But more commonly I carry the spare cast in my damper. Then, if I get into trouble with the one I am using, I have only to remove it and attach in its place the one I am carrying ready soaked between the flannels of the cast box, or stretched around my hat-band.

If one is fishing for trout only and the night is light, there is no need to change from the cast used at dusk. I have often fished throughout an evening and on till midnight with the same cast and fly. One can, of course, use a slightly stouter cast, and if the night is dark, a rather larger fly is often an advantage ; but it is a mistake to suppose that trout take only moths at night. After dark thousands of the small flies that hatched from the water during the daylight fall upon the stream, and it is on the dead bodies of these that the trout feed. The proportion of moths falling upon the water is, I believe, quite small. The small flies are quite easily seen by the trout, as they are silhouetted against the sky.

If one is fishing for sea trout, or if it is known that there are sea trout about, it is advisable to have a slightly stouter cast and a slightly larger fly. Very often the bag is a mixed one, even if one is fishing solely with the idea of getting sea trout. I remember two nights at the same pool on consecutive Saturdays. I was after sea-trout and was using a medium Claret and Teal fly. On the first Saturday I had seven sea-trout and five brown trout; it happened to be my birthday, and I had persuaded my family to come with me and have supper by the river and fish till half-past eleven. I think it was the best birthday party I have ever had. On the next Saturday the figures were reversed: I had five sea-trout and seven brown trout.

If sea-trout are about, it is advisable not to fish the still water, and particularly the tail of the pool, until it is too dark to see the bottom in the shallows. Some say that you should wait until you cannot see the second hand on your watch. In short, don't be in too much of a hurry to fish the shallow or still water; you will only scare the fish and lessen your chances of sport later on. The brown trout are not so easily alarmed, but even with them it is advisable to keep to the moving water at the head of the pool till most of the light has gone.

It is surprising what grand fish come out and rove about on the shallows after dark. I used to fish a stretch of water that had a public footpath along one bank. In the day-time one rarely saw a fish of more than five inches long, and people used to wonder why we went there. The water was about three feet deep and quite steady. One fished carefully, casting under the bushes opposite and drawing the fly slightly so as to keep in constant touch with it. Often it was impossible to see the rise ; one felt it. There would be a sharp tug and a smart, careful strike ; then anticipation as the fish rushed off. What was it going to be, a half-pound brown trout, or a sea-trout of perhaps two pounds ? It was not always possible to judge the size of the fish at the first contact. Very often the largest fish gave the lightest tug and moved off more quietly. After a time I began to notice that in striking a sea-trout one felt a more solid resistance than when a brown trout was hooked. The brown trout felt rather like hitting a partly-inflated cycle tyre ; the sea-trout like one blown up tight. I had many a fine fish from that apparently fishless water, and sometimes the weight of my bag was so great that I had to ease the strain on my shoulder by keeping one hand under it as I trudged the five miles home.

Netting is not usually very difficult in the dark provided one plays the fish right out. The fish always turns on its side when exhausted, and the whiteness of the belly is easily seen. Sometimes one finds that the fish is considerably larger than was anticipated. I remember some difficulty with a salmon of five pounds that took a sea-trout fly in the dark, and another nerve-racking twenty minutes with a seven-pounds sea-trout ; but both were eventually landed.

When a mist rises from the water it is rarely of any use to continue fishing. Some say that it is never of any use under these conditions. But that is too sweeping an assertion ; in fishing one never knows what is going to happen. If, however, you fail to move fish when the white mist comes creeping across the meadows, you will be quite justified in blaming your non-success to this.

A full moon in a clear sky is also bad, and this again is said by some to render success impossible. Very rarely

C

it turns out just the opposite. I had a marvellous hour on the Barle once when the moon was so bright that I could see every stone on the bottom of the river. I was using a single Blue Upright on a 4X point. I started fishing at sunset and had not had a single rise throughout the dusk. Then the moon came up over the hill opposite. I thought that this was the last straw, but decided to fish the pool down, as I badly wanted to take home at least one trout. My first cast produced a fish of a pound, my second one of three-quarters, and my progress down the pool resulted in twelve more fish, not one of which was under half a pound in weight. The pool was about fifty yards long and I started at the top and finished at the tail. I don't think I made more than two dozen casts, and it was certainly under an hour between the hooking of the first and the landing of the last. I think it was the fastest bit of trout-fishing I have ever experienced.

If the pool is so situated that one can fish into the light, one can see the rise ; otherwise one must rely upon feeling it. This is not difficult, provided one keeps the fly slightly moving, so that the cast is always perfectly straight.

If I have a companion, I prefer that he should be sufficiently far away to make it impossible to carry on a conversation. One needs to concentrate on the job, and I like the quietness of the night. Also there are so many interesting things to be seen and heard if one refrains from talking. I cannot remember how many otters have passed close to me whilst I have been fishing at night ; one almost put his paw on my foot as he raised his head and shoulders out of the water to examine the strange object standing motionless above him. But I like my companion to be within calling distance in case of emergency ; it is a great help to have someone to attend to the landing when one has to manage a heavy fish. But if you suffer from " jumps " and dislike " things that go bump in the night," you will probably feel happier if your friend is closer to you ; you will still have a chance of seeing one of the night animals if you will both refrain from talking.

CHAPTER XII

WHEN ?

IN the last chapter I mentioned that, being a family man, I had had to take a good many holidays in August, but that August was not an ideal month for trout fishing.

When I was single I preferred to take my trout fishing holiday in April or May. April, May and June are the real trout-fishing months of the year. If you are single, or at any rate so situated that a holiday without your family will not cause domestic upheaval, I should certainly recommend that you go away in April. I do not think that there is anything quite so delightful as to wander along the banks of a stream when the sallow is in bud and the hawthorn is sending out rosettes of fresh green leaves. To get away from town life at such a time is to taste the real joy of spring-time in England. Chiffchaffs and willow-warblers haunt the hazels and bramble bushes ; swallows and martins skim over the meadows ; and the first cuckoo calls from a thorn tree on the hill-side. You may hear and see many of these things later in the year, but it is their first appearance that has such a heartening effect. Throughout the day a few flies hatch out at intervals and, though the rise may never exceed half an hour at any time, it may be repeated at least half a dozen times during the day ; the best rise probably coming on just before midday.

At this time of the year there is nothing much gained by starting particularly early, nor is much lost by stopping as soon as the sun gets below the horizon. The hours when it is most pleasant to be out are also the most profitable hours in which to fish. There are, however, exceptions to this rule, and I have on several occasions caught trout in April when it has been snowing. One memorable day I was returning homeward with an empty bag at about four o'clock in the afternoon when snow began to fall. I thought I saw a trout rise amongst the dimples made by the falling flakes. I had reached the last pool that came within my rights. I thought I would try to catch that one fish, just to have something for my miles of walking and hours of fishing. I caught it and, whilst landing it, saw two more rise in the same pool. The snow was now falling so thickly that the opposite bank of the river was quite obscured. I caught one of the two trout I had seen rise and then decided to fish back over my tracks a hundred yards or so. I took eight more trout before five o'clock and then packed up, well pleased that I had turned a blank day into such a successful one.

Another April trout has become a landmark in my angling life. We were living on the borders of Exmoor and the river Barle ran just opposite the house. My son had been born but a few days, and the doctor said that my wife might have fish for lunch. We had been snowbound for weeks and there was not the slightest chance of buying any fish in the village. The only thing to do was to try and catch one. I took down my rod, crossed the road, and, standing in two feet of snow, caught a half-pound trout at the first cast. Could anyone forget a trout caught under such circumstances ?

On a mild evening in April I have known trout rise freely well after sunset ; but this has been usually when they have been rising well during the day, and I have not come to the water till a late hour and so have stayed on to make up for lost time. If you have been fishing all day there will be very little object in staying late on the off-chance of a good rise, and so perhaps over-tiring yourself and spoiling a good day on the morrow.

Should you be compelled to take a holiday in March, as I have had to on occasions, do not despair. Not only are there often bright, warm days in March, during which it is a pleasure to be out fishing, but even on the less inviting days there is a pleasure to be got out of the exercise of fishing and walking beside the river. The fish you catch will not be in such high condition as they will be even a month later, and some may be so thin as not to be worth killing. They will not fight so strongly, nor will they be found in such swift water. But against this one must set the chance of hooking one or two of the cautious old rascals that rank as really big fish in their particular river. I think these big fish are hooked or missed once only during the year. Hunger makes them over-eager and incautious during the earlier part of the season ; but if you miss the chance of getting them now it is unlikely that you will get another opportunity later on. Even if you do not come across any fish of heavy weight or strong fighting qualities, the general run of rather weaker fish may be quite enough for you to manage as yet. Every season I start with the same fatal over-eagerness and every season I lose a fly in one or two fish that I should certainly have caught a month later. The expected rise somehow comes as such a surprise that the strike is much too hard. The gut will stand the strain when the fish is only an inch above the size limit, but the three-quarters-of-a-pound fish is too much for it, and I am once again full of regrets at my lack of self-control.

In May the trout are coming into their most perfect condition. The days are long and the weather usually pleasant and warm enough to allow one to enjoy either exercise or laziness out of doors. One can choose one's fishing hours almost to suit the convenience of others. Whether the time available is morning, afternoon or evening makes very little difference. The best rise of the day may occur in any of these sections, and, if one misses the best, it is probable that there will be several other rises almost equally good. Of all the trout-fishing months May is that one during which we should take advantage of any tricks of the weather. Should the day be breezy, choose the most open spot, where the surface of the water is constantly ruffled. It doesn't matter if the water is almost stagnant, provided the surface is broken by the wind, you may throw a fly on to it with the greatest confidence. If there is a fish within a yard it will almost certainly come up to the fly, and you may get half a dozen fish from one good stretch. In July it would be just a lucky chance if you managed to get one trout in such a place, even with the water disturbed by the wind. If the day is warm and fine, fish the steady glides beneath the bushes, and if you see fish rising always take the lowest one first. Fish rising in such places usually have very clearly-marked areas in which to feed and beyond which they do not stray. By taking the lowest fish first you are less likely to disturb those rising, perhaps only at intervals of a yard each, higher up. On a May afternoon I came to a favourite stretch of the river to find five fish rising in just such a situation as I have described and spaced at regular intervals over a distance of five or six yards. I started with the lowest, caught three, missed one and scared one. Had I started with the top fish, I might have caught it, but it is unlikely that I should have caught any of the others.

June is every bit as good a month as May. In many districts it is even better : it is very largely a question of the weather. In any case, it is unlikely that it will be so hot as to make fishing too much like hard work. I have never had a June holiday, but I have fished many an afternoon and evening in June and know how pleasant it is and how obliging are the trout—usually.

July has been spoken of as " impossible " from the trout angler's point of view. I agree that it is, on the whole, the worst month of the season ; but I would not refuse to go trout fishing in July because of this, nor would I object to taking a holiday in this month if nothing better offered. Glancing through my fishing journal, I see rather a high percentage of blanks occurring during this month, but I also see quite a reasonable number of satisfactory days. It is not a month in which you can go to the stickles and heads of the pools and fish with a reasonable prospect of getting a trout ; you must search out the trout, and if they themselves are not in evidence, search out the places in which they are most likely to be found. In July it is generally possible to get a trout or two if one concentrates on the white water at the foot of large stones and rocks. Such water is well aerated and good trout often take up positions in such places, even though the water is only two or three inches deep. My best basket on the Tavy, so far as weight is concerned, was made on a broiling July day with the water at its lowest and clearest. I used a fairly large fly and fished only the white water, always keeping as far away as possible.

August is not a good month for trouting during the day, but there is usually an excellent rise just after sunset and the fish often continue feeding until midnight. During an August holiday I do not bother to fish very seriously during the day-time, unless there has been a nice rise in the river or the water is coloured ; but I do a good deal of observing, both of the situations occupied by trout and the surroundings of the various pools. By doing this I prepare myself for fishing in comfort when the light begins to grow dim. It is a mistake to go to a pool at dusk without having made some sort of examination of the place during daylight ; it may even be dangerous. Also, distances in a dim light are very deceiving ; the overhanging branches that fringe the opposite side of the pool may seem very far away and their closeness is not discovered until you find yourself hung up in them. The same applies to the trees behind you. Half an hour spent in examining the place in daylight may mean all the difference between an enjoyable hour or two after dark and a period of utter misery, lost tackle and temper, and perhaps even a broken rod.

September is often nearly as good a month as any. Trout often feed almost as ravenously as in the earlier part of the season, and for some reason often seem to lose a good deal of their caution. My explanation of this is that many of them are beginning to move upstream for spawning purposes. They have remained in one spot throughout the earlier part of the year and have learnt how to distinguish between the natural and the artificial fly chiefly by the way in which it comes to them. In leaving their old haunts they, perhaps, think that they have left the angler behind them. Their intelligence can scarcely be expected to tell them that the angler can follow them everywhere. This is the only thing I can think of to explain why it is that in September, and particularly towards the end of the month, it often happens that one can take trout freely in places which have been hardly worth fishing since May.

If your holiday falls in September, don't get the idea into your head that other people before you have taken the best of the fishing and that what is left is hardly worth going after. I have had more surprises in September than in any other month of the season. The unexpected may always happen in fishing ; but it is more likely to happen with trout in September than anywhen. Besides, in rivers visited by sea trout, there is more of a chance of hooking one of these by daylight in this month than at any other time. Give me a warm day, a moorland stream running down from a flood and still tinged with peat, and I'll ask for nothing better. The chances are that I shall have hooked at least one really heavy fish before the day is out and I may have caught one, or even more, sea trout. Here is a sample afternoon of September some years ago. I reached the water at about half-past two ; it was running full and with a definite hint of colour. I put on a medium-sized Coch-y-bondu and fished upstream. I fished for two hours and a half and caught four good trout and a sea trout of just over a pound. I also missed at least a dozen brown trout, four sea trout, and two salmon. I was fishing very badly and ought not to have missed so many fish ; perhaps I was rather over-tired after a heavy week's work. One could scarcely call that a dull afternoon ! I had asked a friend to come with me ; but he said it was not worth it. A man must be hard to please who is not satisfied with that amount of excitement in one short afternoon. Two years ago my best catch for the season was on the 28th of September ; it included two fish of a pound each, the average weight for the water being four ounces.

CHAPTER XIII

WHERE ?

IN settling upon the place I intend visiting for an angling holiday there are two things that I consider very important : the fishing and accommodation must be cheap and the scenery must be interesting. The first point is understandable ; you may wonder what scenery has to do with it. It is unusual in a short holiday to get good fishing weather throughout. I am never happy unless I am doing something and to moon about on a holiday waiting for the river to get into some sort of condition for fishing would be absolute misery to me ; so I try to have scenery of an interesting nature at hand, so that, when the river has nearly stopped running and everyone except fishermen is rejoicing in the lovely weather, I also can rejoice because I have some delightful country to walk in and sketch. Fortunately most trout fishing of the cheaper kind is to be found in extremely beautiful surroundings, and I have come across a great many places in the British Isles that have fulfilled both my requirements.

Many people prefer to return again and again to some favourite spot. It is a good plan ; you get to know the peculiarities of the water and the inhabitants. In course of time the place becomes a sort of holiday home. It is so pleasant to be welcomed at the station by the same old porter. " So you be come down again, sir, to ketch a few trout. Pleased to see 'e, sir, and I 'opes you'll 'ave some good sport. Stoppin' at Mrs. Briggs' ? All right ; you go on, I'll bring along yer bag as I come up along." I thoroughly enjoy going to a place where I am known and revisiting scenes of former adventures. At one time I always went to the same place : a little cottage standing all alone beside a Dartmoor stream. I loved that place and got to know it so well that I could walk about anywhere along the rocky tracks without trouble on the darkest night. Then, for family reasons, I went to a place in Cornwall, and this eventually became so well known to me that I could go at once to the right places according to the state of the water and weather.

But at length I felt that I should learn more about trout fishing if I changed the place of my holiday each year, and I should at the same time be getting a wider knowledge of my own country. I knew that I should come across a few worthless places and perhaps on the whole catch less fish than if I had gone back to my favourite and well-known spots ; but catching large numbers of fish is not by any means all that there is in trout fishing. So I visited different parts of Dartmoor, Exmoor, North and South Wales, the Lake District, Scotland, and Ireland. In all these places good trout fishing and comfortable living can be obtained at reasonable prices.

After one or two experiences I have decided that hotels

catering specially for anglers do not suit me. I have nothing to say against the hotels themselves; generally they are very comfortable, and many have their own water close at hand, which is a great convenience. But I have found almost invariably that there is a competitive spirit amongst the anglers one meets in such places, and this I absolutely abhor. They all seem to want to find out what you have done; so as to be able to tell you how much better they themselves have fared in their sport. Much of the same sort of thing goes on in many of the hotels in the regular health resorts. The inmates of these establishments buttonhole you at the earliest moment every morning to enquire after your health, which they do merely to give themselves an opening to tell you at length how terribly they have suffered throughout the night. Unfortunately I have had to stay in such places; so I know. If you want to enjoy your sport without odious comparison with the sport of others, stay at a farm-house or cottage. By doing so you will probably find it much easier to arrange your meals so that they do not clash with your fishing. Hotels cannot always do this; where perhaps two or three dozen people have to be considered, it is obvious that meals have to be at fixed hours, and, if you do not turn up at the right time, you must expect to go without. If you cannot find farm-house or cottage accommodation, the small country pub is often a very comfortable place at which to stay and it is generally possible to arrange for the use of a private sitting-room. But, wherever you go, find out first, if possible, just what amount of liberty you will be allowed with regard to meals; it is a dreadful ordeal to turn up late for an evening meal and get black looks from the staff and silent reproaches from the other visitors. Having once offended, you will henceforth tear yourself away from the water just as the trout are beginning to rise, and, though outwardly you may be at peace with your neighbours, inwardly you will curse them and their rules for breaking in on your innocent enjoyment and yourself for your want of foresight that placed you in such a predicament. Find out also if it is customary to dress for dinner and avoid such a place at all costs ; your holiday is far too short to allow you to waste an hour a day in dressing up. If you want to have a really pleasant fishing holiday, the freer you are the better your chance of enjoying yourself.

In some cases the " free fishing " mentioned in the advertisement of a farm-house, or other place, open to receive visitors is nothing but a fraud. I know such a place to which many have come with dreams of uninterrupted fishing close at hand, only to find that it consists of a miserable little brook scarcely a yard wide and almost dry in summer. About two hundred yards of this brook are available to visitors and I don't suppose there are ever more than six sizeable trout in this stretch. It is almost impossible to cast a fly on any part of it, and the only chance of getting a fish is to dangle a worm in an eddy during a flood.

If I do not know the place to which I am going, I get a map of the district and then enquire what rivers and what parts of them are available for fishing. It sometimes happens that the fishing is three or four miles away. Such a place would be of no use to me : I haven't a car.

I think I have been lucky in that I have never yet been landed at a place where the fishing was absolutely rotten. Perhaps this is partly due to my practice of getting well-forward with my enquiries. I do not mind sending several stamped addressed envelopes for replies to my rather searching enquiries. It is worth taking a little trouble to avoid disappointment and, if the parties won't take the trouble to answer your questions, you may reasonably assume either that they do not wish to disclose the nakedness of the land (or water), or that they are only after your money and will give you as little as possible in return for it. Though an illiterate person may find it difficult to write a clear answer to your questions, she may prove to be an excellent holiday landlady whose first consideration will be to make you happy. I have found many such.

Quite obviously I cannot give you addresses that would be of any value ; now would it be of much use if I named particular localities. In both these matters conditions may change from year to year. As a general guide one might say that anywhere in the British isles where there are moorlands and hills you may be pretty certain to find reasonably good and cheap trout fishing. Of course you must not expect to get a look-in on the really famous rivers ; most of these are retained by the owners, or let off at high figures for the salmon fishing and, though a visitor to the district may sometimes obtain a day's trouting by kind permission of the owner or lessee, it is not much use hoping to spend a holiday there unless you happen to be a personal friend of one of these lucky people.

My best friend has often been the village postman. I have looked on the map and have decided that I should like to fish somewhere in the neighbourhood of a certain village ; so I have sent off a letter to the local postman, enclosing a stamped addressed envelope for reply and a Postal Order for half a crown for his trouble. In my letter I have asked him if he can give me some addresses and some information as to the fishing to be had. It is astonishing what a number of village postmen are anglers.

Where to Fish is an excellent publication and is kept reasonably up to date. Advertisements will also be found in most of the sporting papers and journals.

I always avoid lake fishing ; partly because more than one day of it in a week would thoroughly bore me, and also because it is generally much too expensive for my pocket. A boat is nearly always necessary, and this has to be hired. The owner of the boat in many cases has to be hired as well, and he will probably expect to be fed. If you can do the whole thing at less than a pound a day, you will be lucky. But I have never been able to afford a pound a day for my fishing, even when on holiday. There are exceptions to this general rule of expensiveness in connection with lake fishing ; but they are hard to come by.

CHAPTER XIV

AGAIN, WHERE ?

IT will not be a waste of time if, when we have decided where we will spend our fishing holiday, we give some thought as to where we are likely to find the fish when we get there. Obviously they will be in the water, if anywhere ; but the most unobservant person must have noticed that more fish are to be found in some parts of a river than in others, and it is up to us to find out why certain spots are more favoured than others.

Two things are essential to the comfort and health of a trout, apart, that is, from pure water ; and these two things are shelter and food. Shelter in required partly as a refuge from enemies and partly as a protection from the continual force of the stream. Shade is also a great advantage ; for, though in the earlier months of the year the trout enjoy being out in the warm sunlight, in the heat of summer they prefer to keep out of the glare and spend most of their time in the shade of bushes and weeds.

Why is it that the pools below bridges and the shallows above nearly always contain a goodly number of trout ? It is because bridges usually provide almost perfect conditions for the trout's well-being. Beneath the arches of the bridge and between the stones there is shade

TROUT BEHIND SUBMERGED STONE

and protection from enemies. The pool below the bridge has almost still water in its depths in which they can rest, and well aerated water on the surface in which they can refresh themselves and seek food. On the shallows above the water may run swiftly and, if this is the case, the trout will usually go there only when they wish to feed. Though trout like swift water, it is impossible for them to stay in it for any length of time. Where there are large stones, pockets, or beds of weeds, with swift water flowing over them, the trout will remain ; because behind or in front of the stones, in the pockets, and behind the weeds there will be very little force in the current. Perhaps a few diagrams will help to make this clearer.

In the first of my sketches a trout is seen poised behind a large submerged stone. This is a very favourite situation and one should keep a sharp look-out for any large submerged stones, particularly in fast water, as trout are sure to lie there whilst feeding. Above the stones the water runs swiftly ; but behind the stone it remains almost still. The arrows indicate how the stone forces the water upwards and so leaves a pocket of still water close behind the stone. A trout in such a position has only to exert itself when it is actually rising to a passing fly; for the rest of the time it can lie in water that is quite still.

A stone that projects above the water also provides good shelter for a trout; but in this case the fish is generally lying close to one side, the side chosen being generally that which has the best stream of water flowing past it. If the stone is large, there are probably trout on either side of it waiting in the slack water close to the streams for any food that may be swept by. My next sketch shows a trout, as seen from above, lying behind a large stone, part of which is above the surface

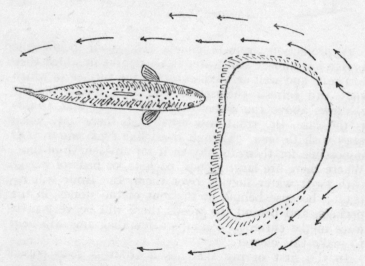

TROUT BEHIND PROJECTING STONE

of the water. A little further down stream the water that has been swept aside by the rock will be flowing less swiftly, and here the trout will lie in the stream itself when they are feeding. Actually most of them are lying *beneath* the strongest part of the stream, though, when they rise, they will appear in the stream itself. There may be a dozen trout feeding in the swift water flowing on either side of a large stone ; but the best fish will probably be in the position I have drawn it— close up to the stone itself.

Water Surface

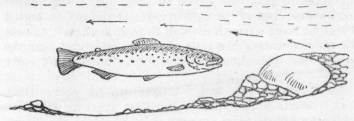

TROUT LYING ABOVE A DEPRESSION

On shallows there are usually certain spots in which you learn from experience always to expect a rise from a trout. These spots do not appear to be different from any other parts of the shallows ; but, if you wade out into the stream, you will probably discover that there is a small pocket, or depression, just where the trout always rise. This depression is probably due to the water sweeping over a tightly-fixed stone and washing out the small stones and gravel from behind it. Small stones may be wedged tightly around the large stone, so that it is almost covered and does not attract one's attention. Trout like to lie at ease in these quiet pockets from which they can dart up at insects passing overhead in the stream. Should you walk into one of these pockets whilst wading, mark it down exactly by some object on the bank and fish it carefully on future occasions ; it will probably repay you well.

Trout also lie just in front of a large stone, whether the stone is wholly submerged or partly exposed. In front of a large stone the water is held almost still by the pressure of the streams above and to the side of it. If water were compressible, there would be a triangular block of greater density than the surrounding liquid lying in front of all fairly large obstructions.

Where water sweeps along by overhanging bushes, trout are sure to collect and may be seen during a rise dimpling the surface all the way down such runs.

Stickles, as the fairly swift shallows and shallow entrances to pools are called in some parts, are always good spots ; but in the earlier parts of the season only a few trout have strength enough to feed in them. It is in the quieter waters, the tails of pools and glides near the banks, that you should seek trout in March and early April.

As a general rule water broken up by rocks, little falls, pockets and eddies is the best type in which to search for trout. The streamy sides of pools, the " run-ins," or entrances to pools, and " runs " or streamy stretches two or three feet deep, are all suitable places. The tails of pools are usually best at dusk or after dark, or when the water is high or coloured. In the spring months many spots, particularly shallows, are swarming with migrating salmon smolts. They will rise every time your fly passes over them. When you find you are amongst these little fellows, fish the deeper water or move to another spot ; you will rarely find trout where they are. Pools with muddy bottoms are rarely much good, but I once found an exception to this in a perfectly stagnant backwater below a mill. In this place weeds were growing quite upright as in a pond. Seeing a trout rise here, I cast for it and caught it. I searched the openings between the weeds and caught several more. For one season that backwater served me well and produced at least one good trout almost every time I visited it ; but for some unknown reason, though I went to it regularly throughout the four following seasons, I do not think I ever took another trout from it. Perhaps the mud at the bottom had become too foul ; or perhaps a large cannibal trout had taken up his position under the mill itself and the smaller trout had learnt to avoid the place.

Still pools are rarely of much use during daylight,

though often providing excellent sport at dusk or after dark. Plenty of trout may perhaps be seen rising in them ; but unless there is colour in the water, or a wind to ruffle the surface, they will be almost impossible to catch during the day.

If you are observant and do not just fish any and all water as you come to it, regardless of its type, you will soon learn to spot the likely places and, what is of equal importance, you will learn how they may be approached

Water Surface

TROUT LYING IN FRONT OF LARGE SUBMERGED STONE

to the best advantage. It vexes me to see a fellow go straight at a place and throw his fly at the water from the first stand he comes to, without making the slightest attempt to examine the place first and find out in what manner and from what angle it can best be approached. Carelessness in handling a river is to me as reprehensible as carelessness in handling a book. Besides, this blundering, hurried way of going to work is quite against the angler's own interests. Much the same rules apply to every river with regard to trout, and what you learn on one stream can always be used with advantage on any others you happen to visit.

I have had some wonderful sport on mill streams, or " leats," as they are called in Devonshire. Those that are swift and shallow are very difficult to fish and, in my experience, do not have many fish in them. But there are many that have very little current in them. They are generally several feet in depth for a considerable distance and probably hold quite a large number of good trout. The best way to ensure success is to keep well out of sight, choose a breezy day and cast with extreme care. The trout in these places are often extremely nervous and dash off up and downstream at the slightest alarm, scaring every other fish in the vicinity. Some years ago I was staying at a farm recuperating from an illness. There was a mill leat passing by the meadows at the back of the house, the fishing in which had been rented by the farmer for the benefit of his visitors. I went there one morning and came back with eighteen beautiful trout. The farmer said that I was the first person to bring back a fish from that leat in the four years he had rented it. I think that the explanation was that, whereas I went to work carefully, creeping

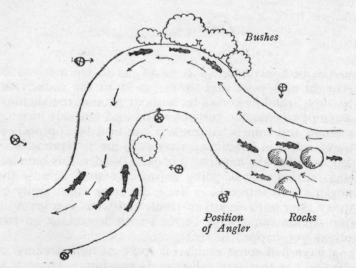

SITUATIONS FAVOURED BY TROUT

up behind the herbage and fishing from beneath the level of the raised bank ; others had blundered along on the path at the top of the bank and so advertised their presence to every fish in the water. One such leat I visit several times each year and scarcely ever without getting some good fish. Often I have to crawl on my hands and knees and peep between the stems of the rushes and sedges before casting. Sometimes I disturb the trout and have to retreat from that particular spot and allow it to remain quiet for at least an hour. These places are frequently so narrow that it is impossible to avoid an occasional hang-up on the herbage of the opposite bank. When this happens, do not try to jerk the fly out by a sudden tug. Shake the line loosely and in many cases your fly will unwind from the blade it has encountered and fall gracefully on to the water, often to be taken immediately by a trout that has been waiting for insects falling from the herbage. If you are firmly fixed, it is often quicker to go round and release it than to break and set up a repaired cast and a new fly. Also, you will have saved your tackle.

The obvious places to fish are not always the best. For one thing, everybody goes to them at once. It is better to take considerable trouble to make two or three good casts in a rather awkward place, and to get a good trout as the result than to spend the same amount of time making fifty useless casts over water that has already been practically fished out for the season.

There was one place which we called " Beginner's Stickle," because everyone started there. And it was just the place for beginners, because it contained no snags or difficulties of any kind. It was a sheer waste of time to fish this place after about the first week in May. But there were two small bays, or nooks, under the opposite bank, difficult to get at by reason of the overhanging trees and the running stream between the angler and these quiet spots. A fly placed carefully in either of these little spots almost always brought a response from a good trout ; but to get the fly there required careful consideration of wind, distance, extending branches and other impediments.

CHAPTER XV

A KNOTTY PROBLEM

"THERE'S many a slip . . ." often far too many ; but we will try to reduce their number by taking care how we make our knots and fastenings.

Gut and gut substitute should be always well soaked before being tied. Nylon, the new synthetic gut, can be tied with perfect safety in its dry state.

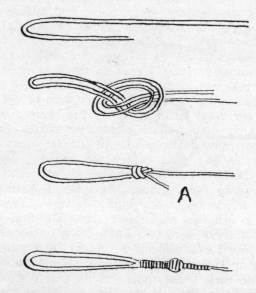

LOOPS FOR END OF GUT AND SUBSTITUTE CASTS

Gut substitute is the most tricky of the three, because it is so much inclined to slip. I never use it tied direct to a hook. My gut substitute spinning traces are tied with loops and, when I use this material for worm fishing, I make a cast with a loop at each end and use a worm hook with a length of gut ending in a loop attached to it. The loops are made by tying an ordinary overhand knot with the doubled substitute, leaving a short length of the shortest end of the gut and whipping down with waxed thread or silk. I use the same sort of knot for the loop at the end of a gut cast ; but in this case I cut off the short end close to the knot.

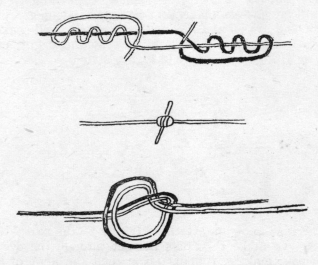

KNOTS FOR TYING TWO LENGTHS TOGETHER

To tie two lengths of gut together the safest knot is the blood knot, which is made by placing the two ends parallel, doubling one end back, twisting it three times round the other parallel piece, and bringing the end out between the strands. Repeat with the other end, pull tight and cut off the ends. But for a trout cast I always employ a much simpler connection and have found it quite satisfactory. In this case the two ends are placed parallel and together tied as an ordinary overhand knot.

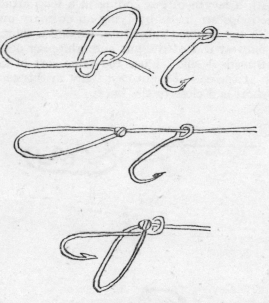

THE TURLE KNOT

The best knot for attaching the fly to the cast is the Turle. To make this, pass the gut through the eye of the hook, make a running noose, pull the knot of the noose tight, pass the fly through the loop, work the knot back to the eye, and pull tight.

A double entry knot is good if the eye of the fly is sufficiently large to take two thicknesses of gut. In this case, pass the gut through the eye of the hook, around the shank, and back through the eye. Make an overhand knot with the short end around the long end, push this knot down to the eye of the hook and pull the whole tight.

A figure of eight jamb knot is also useful for attaching the fly; but it has let me down when using Nylon and also when using a fly with a rather large eye. It is quite safe, however, with real gut when the size of the

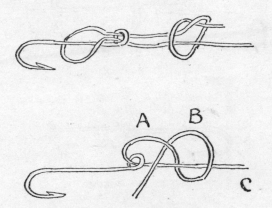

DOUBLE ENTRY AND FIGURE OF EIGHT KNOTS

gut suits the eye of the fly. It is made as follows: Pass the gut through the eye of the hook, turn the end back and around the main gut and back through the loop (A) that is against the eye. Push the eye of the hook back through the loop B, pull on C till the loop B comes up close against the eye, and then pull tight.

Another good knot for attaching eyed hooks is made by passing the gut through the eye and around the cast, tying an overhand knot on the loop thus formed, and pulling tight behind the eye. The result is exactly the same as the Turle knot, though the process is different.

To attach the cast to the line, I pass the end of the line through the loop of the gut, round the gut and under itself. Then tie a knot at the end of the line and pull tight.

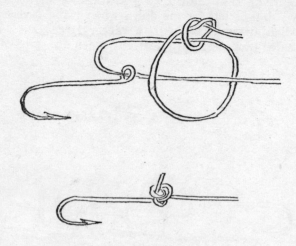

MODIFIED TURLE KNOT

When attaching a fly to a Nylon cast it is advisable to tie a guard knot at the end of the gut, or to use half a blood knot; I prefer the former, but I believe the half-blood knot is quite safe. It is made by twisting the free end of the Nylon three times round the cast, pushing it through the first coil next to the eye, and pulling tight.

To join Nylon lengths I have always found the overhand knot, already described for use with real gut, quite safe for trout. I have not yet used Nylon for sea trout, but when I do I shall use the blood knot. I also use the simple overhand knot for the loop at the end of the cast; but for this I should either double the loop or whip it with waxed silk if fishing for sea trout. In any case, Nylon is inclined to slip more than gut, and it is advisable to test it well after it has been damped.

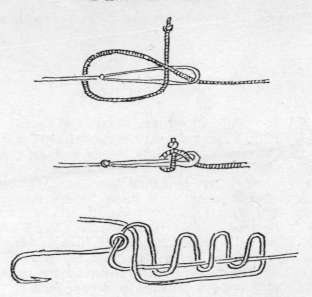

METHOD OF ATTACHING CAST TO LINE, AND HALF
BLOOD KNOT

To whip, bind the silk over one free end. When
enough has been whipped, pass the free end over the
gut or rod and through the loop thus formed. Wind
the free end A three or four times inside the loop, then
wind the loop over this till all the turns of A have been
used up, and pull tight on the free end.

A great many knots have been invented, but those
that I have described are all that I ever use.

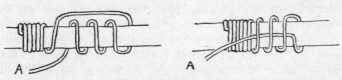

METHOD OF WHIPPING

CHAPTER XVI

FEATHERS AND TINSEL

MY first trout-fishing friend always tied his own flies. To me it appeared marvellous that any one should be able to make such dainty things as trout flies by hand ; and it seemed to me more marvellous still as I watched him tie one as we sat together in an orchard by a Dartmoor stream on a sunny Sunday morning in spring. " I wish I could do that ! " I said. " Why not ? " he replied. " It is quite easy. Here, have a shot at it." He passed me a tiny hook, a length of silk, some beeswax and a little feather. He instructed me in each step, and at length I had produced an untidy lump that it was just possible to mistake for a fly. He laughed at the result, and so did I, but rather ruefully : it was such a different sort of thing from his little work of art. " Might be better, might be worse," said he. " But I'll bet you'd catch a trout on it. Try it." I tied it to my cast and went down to the stream. Sure enough I did catch a trout on it, and was mightily pleased at my cleverness. " You'll soon be able to tie them neatly," said my friend—he was a most encouraging man. Since then I have always tied my own flies, and though none of them are as neat as those I could buy from a shop, and few of them conform to standard patterns, I do not think I have had very unsatisfactory bags as a result, and certainly I have added very considerably to my pleasure by catching my fish on my own flies.

As an occupation for a wet day during a fishing holiday there can be nothing better than making flies. One's thoughts are naturally centred on fishing, and the fact that one cannot at the moment follow one's hobby in

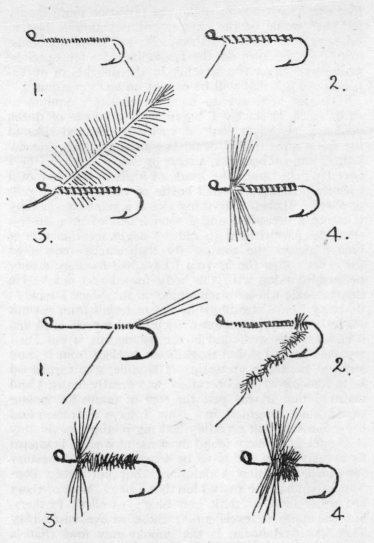

THE STAGES OF FLY-TYING

that direction tends to make the privation more keenly felt than would be the case at ordinary times. But to take out one's hooks, feathers, silks and other materials, and to settle down to the fashioning of a few specials, makes one forget the weather in the delights of anticipating the fish that will be caught on one's creations.

It is not necessary to have an elaborate equipment with which to start. I began with a couple of dozen hooks, a few yards each of variously coloured silks of the finest sizes that I could beg from my lady friends, a small lump of beeswax, a score or two of hackle feathers that I plucked from the heads of fowls in the shop of a friendly poulterer, a small bottle of varnish, and a pair of pliers. Though a fly-tying vice is a great convenience it is not a necessity, and I soon learnt to tie quite respectable flies without its aid. I might mention that it is not always the neatest fly that catches the most fish ; very often the best fly I have had has been a poor bedraggled thing with the body frayed and not half a dozen hackle whiskers remaining on it. Since I took to fly-tying I have steadily collected materials from various sources ; on one occasion a friend and myself unpicked a cushion that we found in the fishing hut of our host, removed several dozen magnificent hackles from it, and stitched the thing up again. The gillie, who turned up in the middle of the operation, was greatly amused and declared that it was just the sort of prank his master would have delighted in. Now I have a tremendous collection that will certainly last my lifetime.

The feather I have found most useful is what is known as a rusty blue. It is to be found on that somewhat rare fowl, the Blue Andalusian ; but not every Blue Andalusian has the rusty blue that I like. Most of them are either light or dark grey-blue ; excellent feathers, but not quite so excellent as those with a rusty tint. The Blue Andalusian is that smoky-grey fowl that is occasionally to be seen in a mixed group of fowls. The head and neck, from which the hackles are obtained, are usually darker than the rest of the plumage ; sometimes almost black. If you see one of these fowls, buy it. The last I bought was on a farm on the edge of Dartmoor. Directly I saw the bird, a somewhat ancient cock, I said " I should like to buy that bird." " Oh, you can't take a thing like that home to your wife," said the farmer. " He's nearly gone past boiling. I'll catch a young cockerel for you. That red one over there is a nice table bird." "But I don't want a young cockerel, whatever its colour," I said. " I want that bird." " But he wouldn't be worth eating," protested the farmer. " I don't care if he is as tough as a board ; that's the bird I want," I said firmly. " It is his feathers I'm after." " If that's all you want I'll soon get you a feather or two," the farmer replied, and at once dashed off after the fowl. He presently returned with two long tail feathers. I had to explain that the feathers I particularly wanted were those at the back of the head and part way down the neck, and that I would not agree to having them plucked from the living bird. After some haggling over the price—he wanted me to accept it for nothing, and I would not agree to that—I eventually got it for a few shillings. That must have happened quite ten years ago, and I still have some of those beautiful rusty-blue feathers left.

This is how I have always tied my flies ; the method may not be perfect, but it has the merit of being fairly simple :

Supposing I am going to tie up some Blue Uprights ; a very useful fly that will kill almost anywhere and right through the season. I first pick out a few rusty-blue or dark-grey feathers, cut off a couple of feet of black silk, and get out a lump of beeswax. I also put out a few hooks of the size I require. I then wax the black silk and proceed to wind this on to the shank of a hook, commencing not too close to the eye and finishing off with a half-hitch at the spot where the bend of the hook commences. If I think that the fly will be better with

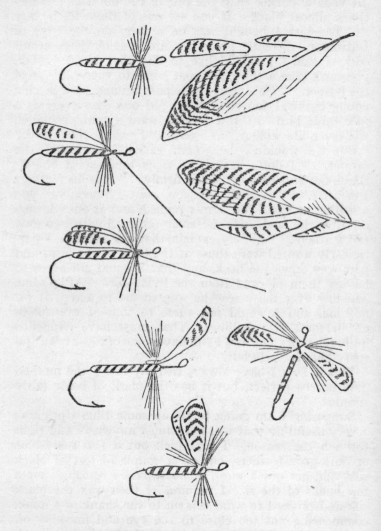

THE STAGES OF A WINGED FLY

a tail whisk or two (the whisk will help it to float if it is to be used dry), I take two or three strands from a large hackle and bind them on with two or three turns of the silk and a half-hitch. I then bind down one end of a piece of straw-coloured silk and wind this yellow silk on to cover the body for about two thirds of the distance towards the eye of the hook, and bind it down by winding the black silk over it in an evenly-spaced spiral (which will produce a pale yellow body with black rings) and finish off with a half-hitch. I then take a hackle feather, stroke it backwards between finger and thumb to make the whiskers stand out, take a couple of turns and a half-hitch round the stem with the black silk, and proceed to wind the feather round the hook-shank. Three turns are usually quite sufficient; it is a great mistake to overload the fly with hackle. Take two or three turns with the black silk around the free end of the feather and fasten with at least two half-hitches. Then cut off the free ends of both silk and feather. Collect a spot of varnish on the point of a pin or needle and drop this on to the head of the fly so as to help fix the fastenings. A small needle with the eye end pushed into a piece of stick makes a fine tool for this job. If I have been careful not to work too close to the eye of the hook, I shall find that between the head of the fly and the eye of the hook there is a little space sufficient to take one turn of the gut when I tie the fly to the cast. This is a very important point; so I take particular notice of how much space I leave, so that, if it is not satisfactory, I can correct my mistake at the next attempt. I then lay the fly aside in an ash-tray or match-box for the varnish to dry, and start the next.

This method of fly-tying, with slight variations, has been that which I have employed for the hundreds of flies and dozens of varieties I have tied. I admit it is not a high-class method, but it works, and that is quite good enough for me.

D

If feather material has to be used for the body of the
fly, as in the Pheasant Tail, Coch-y-bondhu and Palmer
flies, I always spin the feather material on to the tying
silk to strengthen it and render it less liable to be torn
by the teeth of the fish. After securing the stem of
the feather to the shank of the hook, I take the point
of the feather, with the tying silk lying alongside,
and twirl the two together between my thumb and
finger ; then wind both on together and fasten off with
a half-hitch.

The body of the Pheasant Tail fly is made from two or
three strands of the long tail-feather of a cock pheasant ;
the strands being turned lower side outwards to expose
the bronze-red colour.

The Coch-y-bondhu body, and the bodies of most
similar flies, are made by spinning a peacock herl in the
same way as the pheasant tail. The herls are the strands
with short bristles that are found on the stems of the
eyed feathers.

The palmer flies have hairy bodies which are made by
binding on a hackle at the back of the hook, spinning it
on to the tying silk, and winding it along the shank of
the hook.

A woolly-bodied fly may be made either of mohair, or
from the short fur of some small animal : a mole, water
rat, the face of a rabbit, the ear of a hare. The fur is
fed on to the waxed binding thread in small quantities
as the thread is twirled between finger and thumb, and
bound on to the hook at the same time. If some of
the strands are too long, they can be trimmed after the
fly is finished. It may sound difficult ; but in practice
it is quite easy.

Thin silver tinsel adds greatly to the attractiveness
of the fly and is usually wound on in an even spiral with
spaces between the turns. On dark days, or in coloured
water, this ribbing of tinsel gives a flash to the fly that
distinguishes it at once from any drifting oddment.
For heavy water a fly with an entirely silvery body is

often very killing. In this case the tinsel is wound on without any spacing between the turns. A silvery " tip " is said to suggest a fly laying its eggs and is certainly good. It is made by putting a turn or two of tinsel right at the tail end of the fly. The same idea is carried out in the case of the Half Stone and certain other flies, except that the appropriate portion is made with silk (yellow in the case of the Half Stone) instead of tinsel.

I never use winged flies, except for sea trout. To make these I merely add two pieces of selected feather to a fly built as an ordinary hackle fly. But in making a fly to which wings are to be added, care must be taken to keep the hackle well back from the eye of the hook, as additional space has to be found in this case for the bases of the wings. Each wing should be attached separately and the binding should cross over in the form of an X between them. If the wings are to stand up straight, they should be bound on pointing towards the eye of the hook and then pushed back with the thumb-nail and fixed upright by a turn or two of tying silk close up to them in front.

The most useful hackles to have are, first, the already-mentioned priceless rusty-blue, then various shades of grey, red, yellow, and some black. " Badger " hackles of all shades are also very useful ; they are those feathers having a black centre and white, or coloured, edge. White hackles, which you can dye in many bright shades, make very pretty flies. I don't know that they are any the better for their good looks ; but they are interesting to make and cheer one up with a ray of hope when the trout refuse to have anything to do with the more sombre-coloured varieties.

I admit that the information I have given you on this enthralling hobby is extremely scanty ; but I have done this with a definite purpose. I have always had great fun inventing queer types of flies and making up my own dressings of recognised types, and I don't want you to be deprived of the same pleasure. The curious thing is that many of my dressings of recognised types, though extremely simple and differing considerably from what one might call the " correct " style, seem more successful than those tied strictly according to the rules. It is a great thing to have confidence in your fly, and I have a great deal more confidence in those I tie than in any of the very few I have bought. Of course this may be just conceit.

Having got over the initial difficulties of handling tiny hooks and making neat finishes with delicate materials, you will find it much easier to plunge into the intricacies of fly tying as a specialised art, if you are so inclined. I have never had time to get beyond the elementary processes I have tried to describe for your benefit.

In tying the smaller sized flies it is better to start winding on the hackle from the point end of the feather, as the stems of the feathers are rather too thick to wind neatly. It must be remembered, though, that the stem is the strongest part of the feather and it is because of this that I always tie from the stem end whenever possible. To make a neat job of a small fly is sometimes pays to strip off the hackle from one side of the stem.

CHAPTER XVII

MAKESHIFTS, PERHAPS ; BUT NONE THE WORSE FOR THAT

ONE should always have some sort of a repair outfit handy when on a fishing holiday. Mine consists of some strong silk, strong thread, adhesive tape, and a pair of scissors. That is the minimum. It seems trifling ; but it meets all ordinary requirements. When I started trout fishing adhesive tape had not been thought of, or at any rate it had not come my way. The first time I came across it as an angler's accessory was when I called on a friend who was spending a fishing holiday in my neighbourhood and saw him put up his salmon rod. The rod was in three pieces and without furrules. He merely put the sliced ends together and wrapped the adhesive tape tightly round them. " Is that all you do ? " I asked. " That is as strong as a one-piece rod ; perhaps stronger," he replied. " I shall not need to touch it till I go back at the end of my visit. Then I shall just unwind the tape and put the rod back in its case— a five-minutes job." I have had only one break that required a temporary repair since then, and that only to a light trout rod ; but it stands to reason that if the tape is strong enough to hold together a twelve foot salmon rod it is good enough for any ordinary repair work.

A break in a solid wood rod is easy to put right. The broken ends should be shaved off on opposite sides, so that they fit closely together, and then bound together with the adhesive tape. My earlier repairs were made by glueing and binding with strong waxed thread ; but, though I still carry the thread with me, I believe the tape alone is quite sufficient.

As with many things in connection with fishing, there is scarcely any limit to the number of articles one might include in one's repair outfit that might come in useful. But the very thing you wish to find is always the most elusive amongst a vast collection, and the few items I have enumerated will carry you through ninety-nine of the one hundred possible accidents that may befall you, if you live long enough and have a sufficient number of fishing holidays to enable you to reach that stupendous total.

But, besides repairs, there are many odds and ends you can make for yourself, thereby keeping down your expenses and adding to your pleasure by using articles made with your own hands.

Sometimes a net is lost, left behind, or forgotten. It is possible to produce a very satisfactory net out of string and a forked stick. I used such a net for six years. It cost me a few pence only and was as satisfactory as any of the more expensive nets I bought at various times.

Select a stick with a straight stem and a nicely shaped fork. A good bow-shaped fork can often be obtained by cutting out the centre branch of three, a growth that is often found in an ash hedge. The handle should be at least three feet long and the arms of the fork at least one foot. Holes are bored through the ends of each of the forks and a leather bootlace threaded through them. A hole is also bored through the handle at about the middle of its length and another bootlace with a loop at the end passed through this. The net is threaded on to the two forks, the first bootlace is put through the remaining meshes along the edge and made fast to the forks, and the net is suspended over the left shoulder by passing the loop of the second bootlace over a button on

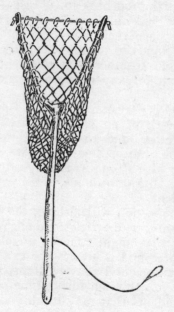

NET MADE FROM A FORKED STICK

or under the lapel of the coat. A net slung in this manner is out of the way till it is required to do its work. It comes to hand readily and is as readily disposed of when not required ; as it is unnecessary to take it from its button, except when one has to reach out a considerable distance. If the opening of the net is rather small for the gape of the fork, it may be found difficult to thread it on to the frame. In this case it can be attached by passing a length of strong string through the meshes and round the forks, knotting it each time it is passed through a mesh.

Another very simple article that can be provided for next to nothing is a cast-damper. All that is required is a flat circular tin and a few circles of flannel or felt. If the flannel is thin, it is an advantage to stitch two or three pieces together so as to form a pad. Single pieces of thin flannel crumple up and are a bother to unfold when a cast has to be removed.

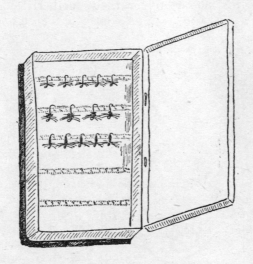

A CIGARETTE-TIN FLY BOX

An effective fly box can be made out of a cigarette tin by fixing pipe cleaners across. The ends of the cleaners only should be fixed to the bottom of the box, seccotine being quite suitable for this purpose. The thick type of cleaner is best, as it appears to hold the hooks more securely. The points of the hooks are merely slipped over the cleaners, the springiness of the chenille being quite sufficient to keep them in place.

Some years ago I got a watch repairer to make me a couple of dozen minnows from a piece of copper tubing. The tubing was cut into various lengths of an inch to an inch and a half, and metal fins cut from a piece of sheet brass were soldered on. The hook-flight consisted of a swivel attached to a piece of strong gut, on which a bead had been threaded to prevent the minnow from sliding down on to the triangle which was attached to the other end of the gut. I painted some of these minnows; but have since come to the conclusion that they are just as effective without further decoration. I

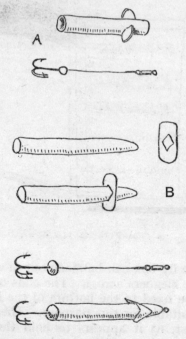

TUBING (A) AND GOOSE-QUILL (B) MINNOWS

prefer these minnows to any I have bought and think that part of the secret of their killing power is that they enter the water with scarcely any splash, and consequently do not set up vibrations alarming to the fish. Many times I have had a trout take one of these minnows as it fell, just as if it were coming at a falling insect.

Another minnow, which is particularly good for low-water conditions at night, is made from the end of a goose quill. The hook-flight is the same as that used with the tubing minnows, and the fins are made from a small oblong piece of metal (part of a cigarette tin will do) slipped over the pointed end of the quill. After cutting out the oblong piece of tin, it should be bent in the middle and a small triangular piece nipped out. When the piece of metal is again flattened out, the aperture is in the form of a diamond and the sharp edges of this bite into the quill and hold the fins in place. The fins are then bent and trimmed until they are of the right size and in the right position to spin the bait. These quill minnows should not be used at the start of fishing a pool at night, as rising trout are liable to be sent down by them when the water is clear ; but, when one has fished out a pool with the fly, it is a good plan to put on a quill minnow and go over it again. I have by this means taken many a big trout that would not have come to a fly.

A fly-lure is also good for the large, non-rising fish, which are usually confirmed cannibals. It is made by attaching three hooks to a piece of stout gut, the middle hook being placed so as to face in the opposite direction to the others. They can face three ways if you prefer ; but then the lure is awkward to fit into a cast wallet ; mine being always carried with the cast already attached, so that I have not got to worry myself with that in the darkness. The hooks used should have wide gapes and should be dressed as hackle flies. Silver tinsel bodies make the lure more attractive. Half a dozen strands of peacock spear, or a couple of badger hackles are attached

to the head of the first hook. These spears or hackles
should reach to the bend of the last hook and, if they
show an inclination to stand up, it is a good plan to fasten
their ends to the bend of the last hook. The lure is
cast as a fly and worked across the pool in a series of
short jerks. It is particularly good at night in brackish
water, where I believe it is mistaken for a shrimp. I
cannot imagine what it is mistaken for in quite fresh
water ; but big trout often grab it savagely.

Good sport can sometimes be had in quite small
brooks by drawing a small minnow made of wood close
along under the banks and round the stones. The
advantage of this wood minnow is that it enters the

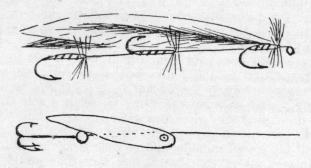

LURE AND WOOD MINNOW

water silently ; the disadvantage is that it is extremely
difficult to cast it any distance. The minnow is made
by shaping an inch-long piece of wood so that one end
is blunt and the other sharply-pointed. A hole is then
drilled through the blunt end, which represents the head
of the minnow, and out below the pointed end at a spot
corresponding to the vent. The line of this hole should
not follow the horizontal axis of the minnow ; but
should be on a slant so as to give liveliness to the movements of the bait. The entrance in the head should be
roughly between the eyes. The wood is then painted ;

brown above, shading to pale yellow beneath being as good a colouring as any. The hook-flight consists of a length of gut threaded up through the hole with a small triangle at the end and a bead to prevent the bait slipping down on to the hooks. These minnows work in a curiously erratic manner, darting up and down and twisting from side to side. Theoretically one should be able to cast them as a fly ; but I have never succeeded in doing this and find their most effective use when fished with only a couple of yards of line beyond the rod top and a creeping attitude adopted as one sweeps the bait along past the likely spots.

I once met a man who always carried a tiny gaff with which to land his fish. It was made by lashing a hook with a gape of about an inch to a short piece of cane. This man carried his little gaff hanging from the button-hole in the lapel of his coat. It was certainly much easier to carry than a net and I daresay quite easy to use ; but I have an idea that a gaff with a barb on it is illegal on some waters and without the barb I do not think it would be a very safe tool to use with such a fish as a trout.

CHAPTER XVIII

CONTACT AND CAPTURE

LET us assume that the contents of the last two chapters have kept us busily employed during a very wet day endeavouring to make a few flies and minnows. Now that the weather has improved, we will go to the river and try out some of these inventions, at the same time endeavouring to correct some of the mistakes we made in handling the fish that obligingly snatched at our flies. We missed a great many rises ; now we will see if we can discover how this came about.

A trout rising in very swift water does so very rapidly ; he is obliged to do so, otherwise the fly would be swept out of reach behind him. In moderately swift water it is not necessary that he should be in such a hurry ; if the fly has passed him, he can catch it with ease, and the current is not so strong that he will lose his balance if he turns across it. In very slow water he can, if he likes, follow the fly and have a good look at it before taking it. These different types of rises must be dealt with differently by the angler. The strike, that is to say the quick turn of the wrist that slightly raises the rod-top and drives the hook in, must be extremely rapid in very swift water. but reasonably delayed in very slow water. It must never be violent ; but should be just sufficient to pull the cast quite straight so that the fish is firmly felt : no more. A violent strike against a heavy fish in swift water will almost certainly result in the loss of the fly. I have heard some people say that in very swift water one should strike as the fish commences to rise. I don't think I ever consciously do this ; in fact, I don't think I could ; but, by keeping the cast as straight as possible, I try to make the strike instantaneous on seeing the rise.

In fishing a slow glide, however, it is obvious that a very quick strike may snatch the fly away from a leisurely-rising fish. One must allow him to close his mouth on the fly and get his head down. This may take a full second of time, perhaps even more ; and a second means quite an appreciable pause between the rise and the strike. The correct timing of a slow strike can only be learnt by experience. I am still learning.

And now, having hooked your fish and found that it is a real buster, you have got to manage him so that the connection is preserved until he is exhausted and can be drawn into the net.

If you have a reel with a fairly strong check, you may have struck " off the reel " ; that is to say, you may have been fishing without touching the line with either hand, in which case the tightening of the strike will have found its resistance in the check of the reel. I use a reel with a very light check; consequently I have to hold the line between the finger and thumb of the left hand and so strike against this resistance. My first care, therefore, on hooking a good fish is to reel up any slack line there may be between my left hand and the reel. If you try striking off the reel with a light check, in many cases the hook fails to penetrate; and, if it does penetrate, the fish in all probability at once takes so much unchecked line from the reel that it gets completely out of control and almost certainly jumps free. I personally should never recommend anyone striking off the reel, because on the few occasions I have done so I have in almost every case lost my fish; but I believe some people are quite successful with this method. If, however, you follow my method of holding the line lightly but firmly between the thumb and first finger of the left hand, you will always have a foot or two of line to give to the fish, if necessary, without having to change hands to bring the reel into operation.

The next thing to do is to keep control of the fish whilst he leaps and dashes about; you must also keep control of yourself. One's natural inclination is to get the fish out as quickly as possible; but over-eagerness often ends in disaster. It frequently happens that a trout when first hooked appears to concentrate its energies in repeated endeavours, by leaps, twists and shakes of the head, to dislodge the hook from its jaws; but start trying to pull hard at the fish and it at once exerts all its strength in an endeavour to get away. When it does this, you run a great risk of having the cast broken by a sudden dash, unless you are in a position to allow it a certain amount of line. The flexibility of the rod itself will provide enough give and take for the leaps and wriggles; but a sudden bolt for the roots of a tree or the shelter of a stone must be countered by allowing sufficient line to permit the fish to get part-way to its intended refuge, but a check sufficient to stop it before it quite reaches its objective. A fish that goes downstream is much more difficult to manage, and requires a much more delicate handling of the rod and line than one that goes across or upstream. Do not attempt to pull a trout up against a strong stream whilst it is struggling. If the water is clear of snags, let it run and continue the fight when it reaches slacker water below. If bushes or other obstructions make it imperative that it should be stopped before it reaches them, try to put on the necessary pressure gradually ; then, keeping the rod fairly well up, maintain a steady pressure until you feel the resistance of the fish slacken-ing. Now, but not before, is the time to start slowly coaxing the fish back until it is opposite you. The main thing to remember during the whole of the fight is that the line should be kept sufficiently tight to hold the hook in the fish ; a slack line may allow a lightly-hooked fish to shake itself free, and too tight a hold may, under the same circumstances, pull the hook out. Care also should be taken to see that the rod-top neither points directly at the fish, nor is allowed to get so high that it fouls the branches of overhanging trees, or that no further raising is possible should the fish make a sudden dash towards your feet ; if this happens, a slack line will certainly result and the hook probably drop out.

If there is a handy shelving beach, run the fish up on to this as soon as it turns on its side, allowing the ground to take most of the weight. Do this quickly in one movement and do not stop the movement until the fish is at least three or four feet from the water's edge. I net nearly every sizeable fish, unless I can beach it. It may not be really necessary always, but I prefer not to take risks. Many a good fish is lost through the hold of the hook breaking as it is being lifted from the water, or the cast getting caught up in some brambles or seed-head. Do not attempt either to net or beach a fish till it shows that it is exhausted by turning on its side.

If the landing net is being used, bring the fish to the net rather than the net to the fish ; and see that the front rim of the net is well below the fish as it is drawn in. I have had more than one good fish knocked off by incompetent but well-meaning friends placing the net too shallow in the water and reaching out at the fish as it approaches, and I have done the same thing myself. Draw the fish well over the outer rim of the net and lift the net straight up (to avoid bushes and other obstructions) and round till it is well behind you. Let this movement be swift and steady, and without pauses. Holding the net above the water to admire the captive is inviting the fish to make one more attempt to regain its liberty ; it gives a frantic leap and is back in the river before you can realize what has happened.

Having got your trout safely out of the water and well clear of the bank, kill it at once before attempting to abstract the hook. This is more humane and convenient than attempting to remove the hook whilst the fish is still struggling. Any trout up to a pound in weight can be killed quickly and easily by breaking its neck. All one has to do is to place the thumb in the trout's mouth and bend the head back at a right-angle against the first finger. Death is instantaneous and merciful. Having removed the hook, press the belly towards the vent between finger and thumb to extrude the contents of the gut, then wrap the trout in a cloth, or deposit on some rushes in your bag or basket. Do not leave it lying on the bank to become dried in the sun or blown by flies ; and at night beware of rats. A friend of mine lost a very good sea-trout which he had left on the bank whilst he continued fishing ; the rats quickly found and removed it.

CHAPTER XIX

IN THE FOOTSTEPS OF THE PURISTS

YOU have no doubt heard something about dry-fly fishing, and in all probability you have gained an impression that it is a very high form of the art of angling, only attained after years of arduous practice and possible only to those possessed of a great deal of leisure and money. It is a very high form of the art, and it does require a great deal of time and study to become really expert at it and to reach anything like a complete knowledge of the subject. But it is possible to attain a fair measure of success and pleasure by the practice of an imitation of this high art, and this without sacrificing too much time or going to too great an expense.

In order not to belittle those who use the dry-fly almost exclusively, and so as not to lay, or even appear to lay, any false claims to the skill and entomological knowledge of the great exponents, I am always careful to distinguish my own methods in this direction by referring to them as " fishing with a floating fly." The true dry-fly angler usually has a special type of rather stiff rod, a tapered line, and an astonishing collection of winged and hackle flies accurately representing the various stages of a great number of natural insects, all of which he knows by name and also at what particular time of the year or day each should be used. We who use a floating fly only now and again when the circumstances are suitable need not bother much about such intimate knowledge. On rocky, swift streams all that is usually necessary is to have a fly approximately resembling in size and colour the particular insect that is in evidence at the moment. I always keep a few rather

heavily-dressed flies of my favourite types and use these
as floaters when I require them.

In order to make a fly-float it is usually necessary to
put something on to it that will repel the water. For
this I use Mucilin, which is a lard-like preparation and
of which I always carry a small tin with which to grease
the first yard or two of my line. A little of this rubbed
into the fly will keep it floating for a considerable time.
You can get bottles of special oil to dab on your flies,
and a tin with a piece of Amadou ; but why add to your
kit when Mucilin will grease and your handkerchief dry
both fly and line ?

A floating fly is usually best when the water is low
and clear and the weather hot. With it one can fish
very much stiller water than one can with the wet or
sunk fly. One casts it on to the water and allows it
to drift over the spots where one expects to find trout,
or where one has seen a fish rising.

A rise to a floating fly is very much easier to see than
one to a sunk fly, because the fish is bound to break the
surface in order to take it.

It is not necessary to use a winged fly. An ordinary
hackle fly will float nearly, if not quite, as well, provided
it has plenty of hackle. At one time the " purist," as
the one who angled exclusively with the dry-fly was
called, would have considered that he had disgraced both
himself and his art by anything other than a winged
fly ; but of late years dry-fly anglers in ever-increasing
numbers are using hackle flies, and have even gone so
far as to allow the hackle flies to sink beneath the surface,
when they call it " nymph fishing." Really it differs
from wet-fly fishing only in that they angle for a particular fish, instead of casting into a particular spot in
the hope that a fish will be there. At one time the
dry-fly angler spoke rather contemptuously of wet-fly
fishing and referred to it as " flogging the water " ; but
now that he has discovered some virtue in the sunk
nymph, and many wet-fly anglers have taken to fishing

with the floating fly upon appropriate occasions, we do not hear so much of this rather silly talk.

To be able to use a floating fly is to add considerably to your pleasure in fly-fishing and to your chances of getting a good fish, when to use wet fly would be very nearly useless. There is no magic or secret about it, nor is there any great difficulty in it ; at any rate not as it is used on the streams you will be most likely to fish. Having doctored the fly so that it will float, all that is required is a little more skill in handling the rod, so that casting is more accurate and splashes less frequent.

It is, by the way, an advantage not to crush the flies you intend using as floaters ; therefore either keep them loose in a separate small box, or see that your fly-box is deep enough to allow their hackles to stick out freely all round. If you use a separate small box, be careful to see that you do not take out two flies at once and lose one in the grass, or that a gust of wind does not scatter them about the country. I remember having one blown into the river where it was immediately taken by a good fish. The creature, having discovered the deception, refused to take another of the same sort when presented attached to gut and line.

Often I use the same fly wet or dry according to each type of water I come to. If the rough water doesn't sink it, a jerk will pull it under. If the next spot is a quiet glide beneath some bushes, I wave the fly a few times through the air to drive the moisture from the hackles, give it a little dab of grease, and it will float quite nicely.

Normally a floating fly should alight upon the water " like thistledown " ; but I think there may sometimes be an exception to this when one is fishing the slack water at the sides of pools when the water is high and coloured. I have frequently noticed that a fly landing with rather a splash under these conditions at once attracts a fish that seemed to have ingored the fly when it pitched lightly and without disturbance upon the water. It may be that the trout did not see the fly until a splash attracted its attention ; obviously it must be more difficult for a fish to see through thick water than through water that is quite clear.

CHAPTER XX

" THIS LICENCE PERMITS THE HOLDER——"

ON all trout licences that I have seen there has been a clause stating that salmon fry (referred to variously as " parr," " gravelling," " smolts," etc.) must not be retained. Many a beginner has had rather a shock when the water bailiff has come along and, having looked into his bag or basket (as he has a perfect right to do), has informed the angler that a couple of his " trout " are young salmon and he will have to be reported to the board of Conservators. On the angler protesting his ignorance, the bailiff probably points out certain not very obvious distinctions and says that he will be let off with a caution on this occasion. But the event has not added to the pleasure of the day. The angler continues fishing, but is in doubt over every fish taken. Yet it is not really very difficult to distinguish between a true trout and a true young salmon. The reason for my use of the word " true " will appear later.

Young salmon are found in two stages in our rivers. They commence life as " parr," and in this stage were for years looked upon as a separate species of fish. This was probably due to the fact that the males develop a milt at quite an early stage of their existence. In many books the difference between young trout and parr is stated to be that the latter have " parr marks " ;

that is, shadowy bluish ovals, somewhat resembling finger-marks, all along their sides. This is a most unreliable distinction. In the stream I now most frequently fish I have taken many trout up to ten inches in length

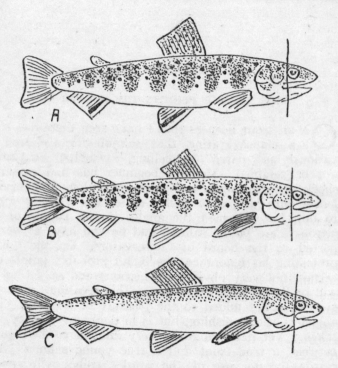

TROUT (A), SALMON PARR (B) AND SALMON SMOLT (C)

which showed distinct parr marks. All young trout and salmon have these marks, though many trout lose them after their first year or two of life. After the young salmon have spent a year or two in this stage, the length of time depending largely on the nature of the water in which they were bred—usually the more acid the water the longer it takes for the young fish to develop—they commence working downstream in preparation for their sojourn in the sea. During this period the edges of the scales grow until all the spots and marks are covered, and the whole fish appears as silvery as a sprat. In this last stage there is not the slightest doubt of their identity, and if you find yourself amongst them, as you may frequently do on a shallow in May, I advise you to get away from that spot at once ; I have rarely taken a trout in the immediate vicinity of a shoal of these little fellows.

But in their parr stage you may meet with them anywhere and at any time, though it is not usual to find trout feeding very freely when the parr are busy. In most rivers the easiest distinguishing features are to be found in the colour of the anal and ventral fins ; that is, the three fins on the underside of the fish. In the young salmon these are colourless ; in the trout they are usually of a yellowish tint, often with a distinct white line and a distinct black line at the forward edge. But in some rivers the ventral and anal fins of trout are nearly colourless and a further distinction has to be sought. The more forked tail of the young salmon is sometimes spoken of as a well-marked feature ; also the longer pectoral fins—the fins that spring like arms from immediately behind the gills. Many trout have forked tails and the size of the fins is not so easy to distinguish unless you can lay two fish side by side. A surer difference is to be found, I think, in the relative positions of the eye and the angle of the jaw. The trout has a relatively larger mouth than a salmon, and this difference is shown by the angle of the trout's mouth being situated *behind* a line drawn level with the rearward edge of the eye, whereas in the salmon the angle reaches only to the level of this line. There is also a good deal of difference between the rise and play of a salmon smolt and a trout. The smolt snaps quicker at the fly and, when hooked, splutters and darts about in a very much more excitable manner than the trout. We may therefore enumerate the following points as fairly reliable evidence that the fish is a young salmon and must therefore be returned uninjured to the water : a quick, snappy rise ; a lively, spluttering, kicking fight ; almost colourless fins beneath the body ; and the angle of the jaw not extending behind the eye.

The usual run of young salmon do not exceed about seven inches in length either in the parr or in the smolt stage ; but I have taken parr of over ten inches and an occasional smolt of over half a pound.

Besides salmon parr and smolt, you may also come across the young of sea-trout and an occasional specimen of hybrid fish. The young sea-trout are often called " yellow-fins " because the edge of the adipose fin (the fatty fin on the back a short distance in front of the tail fin) is marked by a yellow spot, whereas in the trout this spot is red. This is an unreliable feature ; plenty of trout have an orange or yellow spot on the adipose fin. A much more reliable indication of a young sea-trout is the silveriness of its sides. Trout are always more or less yellow on the sides. A silvery fish must always be regarded as a possible young salmon and carefully inspected before it is killed.

Very occasionally, it may be once in a couple of years, you may catch a fish that has the distinctive features of both salmon and trout. This is a hybrid. Until fairly recently hybrids between salmon and trout were unrecognised as such ; but it has now become an established fact that the two species do occasionally interbreed and a start has been made to produce them artificially so as to be able to study their life histories under controlled conditions. You may get pulled up by the Water Bailiff for retaining these fish ; he may assert that they are young salmon and therefore ought to have been put back into the river. I prefer to risk this, because I am particularly interested in these hybrids. I make a careful drawing of every one I catch and make equally careful notes. I do not know what this will lead to ; but that makes it all the more interesting. Anything connected with fishing that widens the interest of the subject I consider worthy of attention. In this particular line I can recall one very interesting incident. I was fishing a wide pool on the Dart and hooked a fish under the opposite bank. My son, who was standing by me, exclaimed as he observed the fish rise and its subsequent behaviour, " Salmon smolt ! "

" I don't think so," I replied. " It isn't a trout ; but I don't think it is a smolt either."

When we took it out of the net we saw that it was an unmistakable hybrid. I made very careful notes of its colouring and markings before putting it into the bag. Then I cast again almost in the same spot.

Immediately there was another similar rise and similar struggle as the fish was hooked. " Another of the same sort, I should think," said my son.

When we examined this fish I noticed several marked differences between it and the first. It was another hybrid, but its appearance suggested to me that it had been to sea. I sent scales from both fish to be read by an expert, giving no particulars other than the date and where caught. When the report came back, it showed that the second fish had, as I had suspected, spent some time in salt water.

Considerable interest may be found in noting the variations in the markings of the fish you catch. In some rivers the trout have a great many more red spots than in others. Some are thickly spotted with very small spots ; others have only a few large spots rather widely placed. In one river with which I am familiar about one trout in every dozen has a very brilliant blue spot on each cheek. In one small stream there was a type of trout, very difficult to catch, that we used to call " canaries " because of their bright yellow colour. These yellow trout seemed to realise how conspicuous they were and would dart away at the slightest alarm. The suggested explanation would of course be that they were light-coloured because they lived in the open ; just as trout living beneath the roots of trees, under rocks, or in very dark streams are usually very dark in colour. But in this case the other trout living in the same open parts of the stream were not nearly so light in colour.

I have caught trout with spots on only one half of their bodies. Some have spots all over their heads ; others, and from the same stream, have no spots at all on their heads. I once caught an almost completely green trout from a stream on the borders of Exmoor. The arrangement of the spots varies ; three spots in a straight line is a not uncommon feature. Why is this ?

A brook trout is such a lovely little thing that it deserves more than a passing glance before it is dropped into the bag. A few minutes spent in examining and admiring the fish is not time wasted.

CHAPTER XXI

END OF THE SEASON

MANY anglers are all-too-eager to start their trout fishing on the first day of the season ; but seem to have had enough of it by the time the dull days of July have come. I prefer to let the fish get into some sort of condition before I start on them and, since July usually proves rather a disappointment, I generally slacken off temporarily for a few weeks about this time. But, when the season is drawing rapidly to a close and the hot, bright days of September are on us, I feel that I have missed something very good that may not be repeated if I cannot spend an hour or two with a trout rod in my hand perhaps on two days of every week of this rich and pleasant month. The fish are in their finest condition, the river is often running well filled, and there is always the possibility on the water I fish of getting hold of a peal.

George had never fished late in the season. He had always been under the impression that it was very little use. An occasional stroll with the rod in the heat of an August evening, more as an excuse for a walk than with any idea of serious fishing ; then the rod had been put away for the winter. But he agreed to come out when I told him that I had caught nine fine fish the week before ; in fact, as good a basket as I had had all the season, though it is probable that I could have exceeded it on several occasions had I cared to do so and if it were not my usual custom now to limit the number of fish taken at one outing to not more than six.

The little stream I fish is somewhat a mystery river in this respect ; you cannot depend on the way in which it will react to the weather. The only thing you can depend on is that, once it becomes well filled, it takes at least a week for it to return to an unsatisfactory state of lowness. Very heavy local showers often have no effect on it whatever ; and, as it lays about five miles from my residence, I can never be sure in what state I shall find it when I arrive on its banks. On this particular occasion a real downpour a couple of nights previously suggested a full and coloured river suitable only for the minnow ; but previous experience advised going prepared for fly as well. George decided to risk it and take fly outfit only. I hate having to look after two top joints ; but prefer this inconvenience to finding conditions entirely against me and with no chance of remedying things. As it happened the water was perfect for fly—a full river that had run clear with only a slight fall in volume. This is a typical September condition.

After looking at the water and turning things over in my mind, I suggested that George should go ahead with the fly and that I would follow with the minnow. I felt that I could cover water he could not and that, by using different methods, we should utilize more fully the possibilities of this rather miniature stream.

What a great delight there is in these last few days of the season ! Every little pool and run has some interesting memory. I have no feelings of regret that it will be six months before I can fish it again. I am grateful to it for all it has given me in pleasures of scenery, sport and country interests during the past six months, and I am filled with a hope, that will not be a disappointment if it should not be fulfilled, that this last day will provide me with the most glowing memory of the whole season. It has happened before more than once ; it may happen again.

In a larger and more open river, with the water in a similar condition, I should have had to confine my spinning to the broken water ; but in many places my little stream flows quietly under thickly overhanging trees. In these dark retreats, by moving quietly and casting upstream, one can spin with as little chance of being seen as in the broken water. In one such place a peal of nearly a pound came at the minnow twice when it was within a couple of yards of my feet. This incident filled me with a great hope. Presently I came to a small, deep pool that has always been a problem to me ; only once have I seen a fish rise in it and I have always thought that somewhere in its depths lurks a large and confirmed cannibal which devours every smaller trout that strays into its dominions. I had no particular feelings of hope as I stood close to the brambles and cast out under the overhanging bushes fringing the opposite bank ; if anything, I believe that I expected nothing more than had happened to me in that particular spot hitherto. At about the third cast a fish took me with a bang that left no doubt as to its species. George was fishing in the faster water above and on the other side of the brambles, but certainly not more than five yards distant ; yet he heard not a sound of the subsequent commotion. Too often in the past have I shouted prematurely, " I've got a buster ! " The gods have looked down and sneered, " Have you, you little blighter ? You wait a bit ; we'll larn 'e ! " Then the dreadful thing has happened and the joy and thrill has sped out of me like air from a pricked bladder. Now I never shout, unless I am in a real fix and must have help of some sort. But I thought he would be bound to hear those resounding smacks as the fish hit the water after each crazy leap and I expected every moment to find him at my elbow offering assistance with the net. He gasped with astonishment as I came round the corner with the peal in the meshes.

The two good trout I had already caught looked insignificant beside this silvery beauty of a pound and a half. I have caught many larger peal ; but few will remain so clear in my memory as will this, the only one of its kind I have taken this season.

Farther along, casting downstream under an overhanging bank, a great head and shoulders appeared out of the gloomy depths as the minnow passed, and I felt a slight tug. I cast again in the same place several times but nothing happened. I think this must have been a salmon ; a peal generally takes with a sudden and very decided bang, a salmon often drifts quietly to the bait. A few salmon manage to get up this little stream every season ; but not once in ten years is one taken by legal means. By indirect channels one hears of occasional salmon taken out on the quiet by means of wire or gaff. I should like to take a salmon in this stream ; but it would be very much a matter of luck if one succeeded in landing one from such cramped and heavily-bushed water. Salmon vary a great deal in their behaviour. In most cases, I think, they appear surprised but not alarmed when first they find themselves hooked. Some never seem to recover from this first rather stupified state and just meander about, with an occasional half-hearted rush, until they are tired and can be landed. Others shake their heads for a time in a rather stupid way ; then suddenly take fright and bolt for it. Peal almost always start to fight directly they are hooked. In this little stream, if a salmon made up its mind to go, one would have a poor chance of stopping it and it would be quite impossible to follow it. I was not really sorry that the fish failed to connect. Had it done so and gone upstream, I might have killed it, provided it stayed in the same pool ; but had it gone two yards downstream, I should have been beaten at once. A rod weighing only a few ounces is not much of a tool with which to manage a salmon in very confined spaces amongst bushes and trees.

Shortly after this we decided to return. Dusk was already creeping over the meadow and the homeward trail wound through many a leafy passage crossed by roots and rocks that required light to negotiate. I don't mind getting about in the dark ; but I don't like risking damage to a valued rod.

I look back on the day, or rather those few hours, with great satisfaction. There is much to be said in favour of the last few days of the season.

CHAPTER XXII

" COME HOSTESS, WHERE ARE YOU ? IS SUPPER READY ? "—(Walton.)

HAVING taught you a little, and only a very little, of how to catch trout—for these chapters could be trebled in number and length and still only touch the fringe of this fascinating art—I cannot do better than finish by trying to help you enjoy the eating of your catch. Good Izaac Walton considered the cooking and eating of his fish a fitting ending to an enjoyable day by the river and, if I take his lead in this matter, I shall be following an excellent example. I should, indeed, be sorry to catch and kill fish, which are in the main such beautiful and lively creatures, if I was not prepared to take some trouble in their preparation for the table and some enjoyment in eating them ; and a trout makes such a delicious meal that it is well worth while endeavouring to bring him to the table in a most palatable state.

The first thing to do, of course, is to remove the intestines. A common practice then is to throw the fish into water and wash it. Walton says of the chub " wash him not after you gut him," and this rule may well be applied to every fresh-water fish, including trout. Having " gutted him," with a sharp pointed knife, slit the thin skin that lies right along below the backbone and carefully remove every trace of the streak of clotted blood that will be found there. In this blood resides all the muddy or weedy taste the fish may have. Now wipe the fish inside and out with a cloth that has been dipped in water and wrung out. On *no* account allow the fish to lie in or be soused with water ; neither remove the skin nor scales. Washing the fish seems to remove a great deal of its natural oils and renders it insipid ; removal of the skin and scales also allows the escape of much of the fish's sweetness. A pinch of salt may be rubbed into the now-exposed backbone, particularly if the fish is to be left overnight. I may add that it is much better to clean fish the same day that they are caught. I am rather fussy on this point and always attend to it myself as a natural part of my job as an angler, and also because I am then sure that it is done properly. The fish is now ready for cooking.

Small trout are best fried in plenty of boiling fat. Larger trout can be boiled and served with a suitable sauce ; or stuffed with a good herb stuffing and baked. Peal should certainly be boiled and served either hot or cold. I am very fond of a cold fried trout with a sprig or two of fresh watercress. In any case, the cooking should be neither overdone nor underdone. Fried parsley is a pleasant addition. But I will not go too deeply into the matter of cooking, as it is probable that that is not your department.

Now you may think that all you have to do is to eat the fish ; but there is an art even in that.

First and foremost, never put the fish upon its back to remove the meat. Most people do this, split the fish right up, and then proceed to sort out from the shattered carcass such morsels of flesh as appear to be, but probably are not, free from bones. The result is a somewhat troublesome meal for the diner and a very inelegant sight for others present. Here is the most satisfactory method : keep the fish upon its side, slip the knife under the skin of the exposed side and turn it back—it will come off quite easily. Now place the knife along the median line, which is the well-marked division between the flesh of the ribs and that of the back, and proceed to push the flesh to right and left from the bones, taking care not to detach the ribs from the backbone. When one side has been dealt with, turn the fish over and proceed in the same manner with the other side. If the trout has been nicely cooked and not dried up, and your part of the performance carried out with care, the result should be that all the flesh has been removed from the bones and a complete skeleton remains. May I add that the cheeks of a well-fed trout are particularly toothsome.

And now, having been with you to the tackle shop, taken you to the river, superintended the cleaning and cooking of your catch, and witnessed your enjoyment of the meal, I will leave you to digest it all ; hoping that, when you sit before your fire, as I am now sitting, after many years of angling in many different parts of the country, you will have as many happy memories to look back upon as I have. And that, believe me, is saying quite a lot.

Angling Ways

by E. Marshall–Hardy *Demy Octavo*

New, completely revised and enlarged Edition.

Profusely illustrated with scores of beautifully executed diagrams, practised anglers will enjoy those features in this book which are quite new to angling literature, while the novice could not wish for anything more complete and concise.

Angler's Creel

by Alexander Wanless *Illustrated.* 8s. 6d. net

The seventh and latest fishing book by the "inventor" of the term "thread-line angling," now universally used. Nature, fish, rivers, methods, experiences, practical information and much else besides—such is the catch in this well-filled creel of generous size.

The Budding Angler

by A. R. Harris Cass 8s. 6d. net

With many illustrations in line and half-tone.

The author, who is both a nature lover and an expert with the rod, relies on the water-side for his inspirations, with the happy result that his writings are both invigorating and informative.

A Fisherman's Notes to his Son

by Norman E. Hill 8s. 6d. net

Illustrated in line and half-tone.

A straightforward account of the methods which the author prefers and has found to be the most simple and effective when fishing for salmon, trout, grayling, pike, and general fish. It contains much sound practical advice and seeks to simplify many of the more complicated aspects of the sport.

HERBERT JENKINS LTD., 3 DUKE OF YORK ST., S.W.1

Coarse Fish

by E. Marshall–Hardy *Illustrated.* 7s. 6d. net

The Field : " Much information which is not readily available elsewhere. . . . Altogether, this is a most enjoyable and useful book
which no angler interested in coarse fish will regret buying."

Tackle-Making for Anglers

by L. Vernon Bates *Illustrated.* 10s. 6d. net

Scottish Field : " All that the amateur need ever know about tackle-
making at home. Almost the first and certainly the best thing of its
kind."

Shooting and Gunfitting

By Arthur Hearn *Finely illustrated.* 8s. 6d. net

The beginner will find this book indispensable, while even the accom-
plished shot cannot but study it with interest and profit. Practically
every aspect of shooting is covered—safety first, cartridges, loading,
marksmanship and the right way to shoot, the shooting position, and
gun-mounting.

Elements of Yacht Sailing

by Alec Glanville *Illustrated.* 10s. 6d. net

" A useful guide to the novice in sailing. The author takes him from
the earliest stages to the time he becomes a competent seaman and
navigator."—*Daily Telegraph.*

HERBERT JENKINS LTD., 3 DUKE OF YORK ST., S.W.1